PICKIN UP THE PIECES OF YOUR LIFE

It is never too early – It is never too late

*To: Seth
Keep on being YOU!!!
Jim*

James W. Johnson Ph.D.

Copyright © 2014 James W. Johnson Ph.D.

All rights reserved. No part of this book may be used or reproduced by any means, graphic, electronic, or mechanical, including photocopying, recording, taping or by any information storage retrieval system without the written permission of the publisher except in the case of brief quotations embodied in critical articles and reviews.

Scripture quotations and references were taken from the Holy Bible, Zondervan Publishing House, Grand Rapids, Michigan 49530, U.S.A. www.zondervan.com

Or

Scripture taken from *THE MESSAGE* Copyright©1993, 1994, 1995, 1996, 2000, 2001, 2002. Used by permission NavPress Publishing Group, Colorado Springs, Colorado 80935

WestBow Press books may be ordered through booksellers or by contacting:

WestBow Press
A Division of Thomas Nelson & Zondervan
1663 Liberty Drive
Bloomington, IN 47403
www.westbowpress.com
1 (866) 928-1240

Because of the dynamic nature of the Internet, any web addresses or links contained in this book may have changed since publication and may no longer be valid. The views expressed in this work are solely those of the author and do not necessarily reflect the views of the publisher, and the publisher hereby disclaims any responsibility for them.

Any people depicted in stock imagery provided by Thinkstock are models, and such images are being used for illustrative purposes only. Certain stock imagery © Thinkstock.

ISBN: 978-1-4908-5538-7 (sc)
ISBN: 978-1-4908-5537-0 (hc)
ISBN: 978-1-4908-5539-4 (e)

Library of Congress Control Number: 2014917938

Printed in the United States of America.

WestBow Press rev. date: 11/4/2014

DEDICATION

To Jesus Christ my Savior and Lord, who changed my life in forever?

My wife Mary - whose love, patience and quiet support were never in short supply.

My Son Peter and Esther my daughter in-law – you stood beside me with positive; loving encouragement, just what every Dad, writer and future author needs.

Eloise and Gabrielle, grand-daughters who made my world one of hope, laughter and are evidence of the power and love of God and the *value of new life*.

Rebecca, my sister, you always encouraged me with your laughter, it was contagious and I caught it.

My parents William L. and Thelma Z. Johnson, my sons Eric and Aaron who were all a part of the story and are all in the presence of Jesus. The memories of you all kept me writing.

CONTENTS

Foreword ix
Preface... xvii
Acknowledgments.. xxi
Introduction... xxiii
From Mary xxvii

PART I

Chapter 1   "The Unexpected" 1
Chapter 2   "Change" 16
Chapter 3   "My Teenage Challenge" 28
Chapter 4   "Signing Up and Almost Signing Out" 42
Chapter 5   "Trusting & Moving" 51
Chapter 6   "The Way Out" 58
Chapter 7   "Back Home Again" 72
Chapter 8   "The Summer, The Wait and the Victory" 81
Chapter 9   "A Family Thing" 99
Chapter 10 "A Unique Opportunity" 111

PART II

Chapter 11 "Panic" 127
Chapter 12 "Anxiety Solutions" 139

Glossary 159
Reference 161
About the Author... 163

FOREWORD

A few years ago I was involved in a project called *Start> Becoming A Good Samaritan*. As the author of the book and curriculum I had the honor and privilege of working with some of todays foremost Christian Thinkers, Authors and Pastors on the subject of what it takes to live out your faith as a modern day Good Samaritan.

Imagine spending time with Philip Yancey, Chuck Colson, Desmond Tutu, John Ortberg, Eugene Peterson, Joni Eareckson Tada, Rich Stearns and Kay Warren (just to name a few) talking about practical, real ways to live like a Good Samaritan. It was insightful, instructive and inspiring. But most of all it was approachable and real!

What does my experience working with these very prominent Christians have to do with writing the forward for Jim's book? I'll use those words again- "approachable and real." When I first started reading *Pickin' up the Pieces* I wasn't sure what to expect. Once I got to about page 30 and fully embraced the conversational, personal journal writing style that Jim uses, I was first and foremost struck by how his stories felt like an old pair of comfortable slippers that fit me, and my life, just right!

Through glimpses into the twists and turns of Jim's life from the spectacular to the mundane, we see how from an early age, when important life moments occurred, he let anxiety, fear, doubt and even at times depression rob him of the joy that could have been. He thought those pieces were gone forever, destroyed by what he calls the "Toxic Crew." But through the saving grace of Jesus Christ and some very practical advice on how to slow down, not live in regret, think before you act, and "Reclaim your Brain" Jim learned how to "complete the loop and reclaim those lost pieces.

To help the reader go deeper Jim also ends each chapter with a series of mental and written exercises that help you take his personal stories and convert them into your own. I found these little exercises to be a welcome and thoughtful addition to the book.

In a curious but appropriate demonstration of God's involvement in our lives, I first met Jim when he approached me to be the keynote speaker for a fundraiser for Guiding Light Mission, a wonderful ministry that serves homeless men in Grand Rapids, Michigan. I remember telling him I thought he had the wrong guy and that I was uncertain if I could comfortably speak to 350 people.

You see one of my big fears growing up was speaking in front of people. All through grade school and High School I would find any way I could to avoid being called on to answer the teachers question in front of the rest of class! So fast forward to 2014 when Jim encouraged me to face my fear and told me that with God's help he was positive I could not only do it, but would do an excellent job! If I hadn't met Jim I wouldn't have had the opportunity to pick up that piece of my life and reclaim it as my own. Perhaps you have some pieces of your life that you thought were gone and never to be found again. *Pickin up the Pieces* will help you close the loop, bring redemption to lost areas of your life and show you that your key partner in this journey of life, Jesus Christ, is there to help you put every piece perfectly into place as he molds you into the man or woman he wants you to be.

Michael Seaton
Author, *Start> Becoming a Good Samaritan*

"WHAT OTHERS HAVE TO SAY ABOUT "PICKIN UP THE PIECES..."

"Jim's honesty and vulnerability opens the door for us to join him on his journey. As you see how your journey parallels his, you'll be led to seriously contemplate the "pieces" of your life. If you've been trying to make sense of the fragments of your life, this book is for you. Don't miss this rare opportunity to learn from someone who's been refined by God through the process."

Doug Redford, *Pastor of Men's Ministry*
Ada Bible Church, Ada, MI

"Jim Johnson's personal account of redemption rings with credibility and authenticity. The lessons of his life, expressed through both pain and joy, will serve as an encouragement to every reader. His experience reflects God the Shepherd's love for the one wandering among the 100 sheep.

Vicki Forester Downs, Downs Consulting LLC.

The faith from this book is water to the thirsty soul and holding on to God's unchanging hand never ceases throughout his personal journey and message. Dr. Johnson takes you to a place of rescue and renewal....guiding and showing all of us by "picking up the pieces" with God's help, you will never lose, <u>never</u>. So take the time to sit back, read and take a drink!

Becky Blocksom, *Recording Artist, Humorist and Illustrator*
From Her Heart Ministry

Jim has done a great job of sharing his life experiences with the reader. Even as a close friend I learned from him in this book. He invites us to peel back the years of heartache, disappointment and discouragement and encourages us to reclaim those times for the glory of God and our own personal healing. His observations and probing questions cause you to think about those difficult times in your own life and then take action on those thoughts and move you to a better understanding of who you are in Christ; and how He can transform who you are into what He desires you to be.

Steve Hilbrands, Friend, Inventor & Entrepreneur

"Pickin Up the Pieces of Your Life" may be like the book you have always wanted to write about yourself. It may be like the story you've always needed to tell those you most love. I met Jim on the other side of his journey of fear and faith, after God "restored the years that the swarming locust had eaten." (Joel 2:25-32. NKJV) Maybe it's God's time to "restore the years that the swarming locust have eaten" from your life.

Denny Cochran,
College Campus and Street Evangelist

This book uniquely captures how Jim Johnson's spirituality became a main source of strength and support during each of his life - changing / life - challenging experiences. Jim invites you to discover how your belief and love of God becomes a dominant Christian lifestyle, especially in overcoming fear, anxiety, and undesirable addictions.

Greg Bauer,
Spiritual Author & Writer
Author "The Breathing Blanket"

Jim's book should be read by those who are seeking direction and purpose in their lives. It should also be read by those who are helping those who may have lost their way. While Jim's unselfish service to the Marines & families of Alpha Company helped him Pick Up a Piece of His Life that had been dropped on his life's journey – it was equally fulfilling and comforting for us as Marines to know that someone had our backs and our families' backs while we were deployed in Fallujah, Iraq. Jim's service to us and our families actually helped turn the tide of history in Al Anbar. Jim's personal stories and 'Things to Consider' give an opportunity for the reader to reflect upon his or her life so that they may too live a more fulfilled life

Lt. Col. Dan Whisnant USMCR
'Former Company Commander of Alpha Company, 1/24, Grand Rapids, MI"

"What should we do when the impact of loss hits?" Jim answers this question and many more that probably plague you, as well as me. Jim provides practical, biblical counsel and opportunities to think and reflect on the "what if's "of life.

Jack A. Haveman, Station Manager
Moody Radio of West Michigan

PREFACE

The thought of writing a book has been a dream and as close as my skin for many years. It was 25 years ago; I was on vacation with my family in Mackinaw, City Michigan. It was then that the idea of writing a book came to me for the first time. I had gone out early to walk and take in the quiet beauty that surrounded me. From where I was standing near one of the piers I could see the Mackinac Bridge to the west and Mackinac Island straight ahead. The sun was reflecting off of the water and there were sounds of human activity as the car ferries were being prepared to carry visitors to and from the island for the day. I remember the feeling of anticipation that was a part of that memorable moment in time. From then on I began to think more about writing a book.

Then, when I ran my first marathon at age fifty-two, I documented the journey in detail hoping to write the book I felt so strongly compelled to write. I organized my notes and writings and attempted to write a book about the experience and how it related to life, but the book was never written. But a journey I began back in 2007 led me to begin writing with focus and purpose and this book is the result of that effort.

After seeing the title of this book, giving a brief look at its pages, the table of contents or even this preface, you may have found something that has earned your attention. It may be the title which gives hope to you in regard to recapturing, picking up something that may have fallen on the roadside of your life. It may be the mention of addiction, stress, anxiety, faith, fear, doubt and even depression the "Toxic Crew" that has gotten your attention. Whatever it may be, I hope reading this book will help you move toward positive change and improvement in your life.

At the end of October in 2007, I was told by my employer to pack up my belongings and depart. I did not realize fully what was occurring except, I was immediately unemployed. At the time, though a bit shocked, I thought this will be OK. I wasn't sure how my wife would react but we had lived a lot of years and life had not been perfect, so I assumed we would be just fine. My immediate supervisor who broke the news to me was a friend and remains so to this day. It was difficult for him to tell me this news, but he did so respectfully and with compassion.

I am unsure what occurred over the next few days because it was different than anything I had experienced before. My throat began to close, I had trouble breathing, I had this very dry cough and I was having trouble sleeping. I could not relax. I was blessed to find two part-time positions over the next 45 days that met our needs financially. But these crazy physical and emotional symptoms continued.

Outside of my family and of course God not many people were aware of what I was going through at that time. Then, one day in early 2009 I happened to be listening to a CD of an interview I had emceed. I didn't like what I heard. I asked myself, why I am I talking so fast? Why did I sound the way I did? Then I began to ask why was I acting the way I was acting? This only increased my desire to learn more about me. This was important and I found that it was OK to see myself in a new light. With God's help I was able to handle the tumult that was inside me. I was getting a sense that the ensuing change that could occur was going to be OK. Based on my real life experiences, I am convinced that most anyone can handle change and personal improvement, if they avail themselves of the opportunity and give themselves the permission to do so.

As you read this book I encourage you to slow down and consider what you are reading. <u>Think about what you are thinking about.</u> You may find as I did that when you think, really think, write a few notes, consider and of course pray about your situation, you may come to the same conclusion I did. You may conclude that the change you are experiencing is good.

In this book I share how I dropped pieces of my life as a result of out of control stress. Pieces are dreams, goals, careers, and relationships, I was able to pick several of them up and I explain what they were and how that all worked out for good. This stress caused anxiety, fear, doubt, and even some depression. I call stress and these ensuing elements a "Toxic Crew." When permitted to have control of our lives this "Toxic Crew" will simply put, "mess everything up." Your life will seem out of order. You may be confused, worried, fearing or dreading certain things that were previously no big deal. You may not sleep well. You may have an ongoing movie of what may or may not happen to you or your loved ones playing continuously in your mind. You may be so anxious it is hard to relax or focus even a little bit.

With that said, just remember, you alone are reading this book. No one is reading it to you or with you. No one can know what you are thinking, unless you choose to share it with them. That is what is wonderful about quietly reading and thinking; only you know for sure what is going on. Then, if you uncover one thing that can help improve your life, you can take action and experience improvement. Someone will notice the change…with God's help, some faith and hope; you may be on a new journey yourself and one that ultimately has a great ending. I hope it is an ending of which you have dreamed. It certainly could happen to you!

ACKNOWLEDGMENTS

So many people contributed to this book by being a part of my life, it would take many pages to mention you all. But I do want to recognize a few of you.

To my good friend Steve Hilbrands who met with me weekly. Your encouragement, honesty and ever challenging input played an important role in the completion of this book. We all need someone who will help us see more clearly and you were that help for me.

To my inimitable friend Greg Bauer, who as a life coach and now fellow author and of course expert listener helped me set benchmarks to complete this book. I will forever be indebted to you and the wisdom you shared with me.

To all of my friends and family members who at one time or another spoke a word, shared an idea, or simply encouraged me to keep keeping on, thank you from the bottom of my heart.

To the members of the small group which Mary and I belong: Paul, Brenda, Bob, Carla, Mark, Ruth, Kevin and Shirley who prayed for me and my family. As brothers and sisters in Christ you stood in faith with me, thank you.

To Lavonne Berghorst who for 12 years, virtually every Sunday at church challenged me to finish this book. You challenged me by simply asking "where is the book?" When I told you it would be done soon, you would say yea, yea. Well, here it is. You may have thought your words were landing on deaf ears, but the Lord used you to make sure I never quit…thank you.

INTRODUCTION

Every person that is born on this planet arrives in a place that has its challenges. You could say, everyone who is born on this planet enters a hard world. I never look past the goodness of God nor the wonderful people who share this planet with me; I do however understand it is a world where darts of hate, envy and strife are aimed at every person at some time in their life. All of this confusion and uncertainty can cause an amplification of stress that can lead to anxiety, fear, doubt and even depression, the "Toxic Crew." This is where our loop begins. It ends many pages later and you will see its closing if you keep reading.

As I was writing this book, I gazed over the landscape of humanity from where I live, breathe and have my being. I know there are many people who have stress in their lives and have let it overwhelm them. This is what happened in my life to one degree or another for many years, beginning when I was a child. They, like me have become anxious, fearful, doubtful and even intermittently depressed or worse, depressed. I have found many people are being medicated for the long term, not just using medication as a tool to metaphorically "get me to the hospital," but making it a part of their life for many, many years. I am not telling anyone to arbitrarily set aside their anti-depressant or any other drug they may be taking. I am simply sharing what I see in everyday life around me. I had the option to take medication, but I chose to work through my life issues differently. You may be able to glean something from my experiences, I hope so!

It is for sure none of us knows exactly what life is going to bring. What is unusual about that statement is that we are often unaware of what is really going on in our lives; and by the time we figure it out, we are caught off guard by the demands of life and the resulting change.

You can experience stress at any age or stage in life. Amazingly, I had been told to relax and or take it easy for many years. I wrote some of this off as my personality and desire to achieve, to win, and to overcome. This book will tell you how I uncovered what was behind the "relax and or take it easy comments."

I have had successes and failures. My life has included times of faith and fear. I have asked myself, who I am in both the bigger and smaller scheme of things. I have asked out loud, WHAT IS MY PURPOSE? There have been times when I asked out loud WHY DID I DO THAT? I simply wondered why I did certain things and felt a certain way, but I never took the time to think about it, consider what was happening or had happened in my life. This book gives some insight into how I learned more about myself.

For certain, each life has experiences that are similar to what others have experienced. I can tell you for sure, that in my life I have had more good things than bad occur, you too? I have made mistakes and offended people, for that I am sorry, you too? I have had people take advantage of me, misunderstand me and a few times intentionally insult and hurt me, you too? I have forgiven them and moved on, you too? I have found that stress, leading to anxiousness, fear, doubt and even some depression has impacted my life negatively, you too?

After giving thought to my situation and doing some serious research I can tell you that everyone has moments of stress. For some the effect is more and for others less and that is an important key in dealing with issues of life and especially those referred to in this book.

I *truly* hope there is something in these pages that blesses you and gives you hope and encourages you to move ahead and not retreat (just in case you were thinking about it) in life. Just remember that in your life you will see and experience stress. Christian or not, anxiety, fear, doubt and even some depression may invade your life. I can tell you that being a Christian helps recognize and resolve these issues. Many of us simply don't recognize what is really going on in our lives, but we must!

This book has two major parts. The *first* includes interesting excerpts from my life story with all of its twists and turns. I also share how uncontrolled stress, as well as the anxiety, fear, doubt and even some depression, the "Toxic Crew" that followed were woven into my life from my youth. I scatter throughout this part of the book five examples of how I was able to pick up pieces of my life that I thought were gone forever. I personally proved that it is never too early nor too late to pick up important pieces of your life that you thought were gone, never to be found again.

The *second part focuses more on the journey I began in 2007. I will reveal and* explain much of what I learned about anxiety. I will demonstrate how with God's help I overcame negative influences in my life. I will provide some strategies that are basic and easily understood that will help you successfully wrestle and win over stress, anxiety, fear, doubt and even some depression.

This book does not encourage you to go back into your life, dredging up the negatives, being full of regret, sorrow, and focusing on what you didn't do, or couldn't accomplish. It is a matter of finding what you want and what you would like to restore, *can restore* or what has already been restored. At the end of each chapter I will provide some interesting points for you to consider about your life. Then you will have the opportunity to think and write a few notes about what is or has been going on in your life. I always keep faith, hope and restoration in Christ at the center of Things to Consider.

Finally, I just want you to know that I am not a psychologist, psychiatrist or counselor and don't pretend to be any of the three or part of a related profession. I also want you to know that this book is not intended to be a scholarly work; I have already written a doctoral dissertation and have no desire to do that again…at least for a while. Neither is it a book filled with the advice from a broad collection of experts. This book is filled with my expressions and real life experiences. I am someone who has lived a few years and found a few solutions to life's challenges that have helped bring restoration to my life…I simply thought I would share them with those who are interested. In this world in which there are so many voices saying so many things that can be so negative and confusing, this book may help bring some clarity into your life, I hope so!

It is my pleasure and honor to have you read my book.

Thank You So Very Much,
James W. Johnson Ph.D.

FROM MARY

As Jim's wife and his partner for almost forty-four years, at his request I read this book a couple of times. I helped him with editing and checking information. After I finished reading the book the first time, Jim asked my thoughts on what he had written. The first thought that came to my mind was, the readers are not going to believe all the things you wrote. He asked me why and I told him, there are so many things that happened to one person and his family it just doesn't seem possible. However, I can tell you it is all true. So as you read this book I hope you will find something that will encourage and inspire you as you continue on your life's journey. I also hope you find the peace that comes from knowing the Lord Jesus Christ.

PART I

CHAPTER ONE

"THE UNEXPECTED"

My birth was unexpected! It was normal in regard to a date, a town, a hospital, and a new baby boy born into a post WWII era in America. However, I belonged to a married couple who *did not expect* me. There, I think that covers the basics. I was born in Tiffin, Ohio on May 3, 1950. My parents married when they were in their thirties with no intention of having children. They were told unequivocally by doctors that it would not happen. Ooops! I came along, and that was not all. Nine years later when my mom was forty-five years old she gave birth to my sister Rebecca.

She struggled with both pregnancies. Many years later mom and I discussed her pregnancies and her struggles. We agreed that Becky and I being born caught them totally off guard, and had something to do with the plan of God for their lives. I firmly believe that serving God is not about behavior modification, man's medicine, sociology, social work, psychology, biology, or anthropology. He has a plan and it is the Gospel of Jesus Christ.

James W. Johnson Ph.D.

It is a great, powerful and comprehensive plan for our lives. It is wonderful to know that you are a part of a detailed plan that is intended for good.

Everything has a beginning. Regardless of your age, you can remember some kind of a starting point in your life. Were you three years old when you first remembered an event or maybe four or five? Regardless, there was a time when you can remember something happening, and that is where you first began thinking about this life. I have really great memories of my early years in Sycamore, Ohio. I believe it is safe to say that I first remembered things in my life at about age three. When I was six we moved from Sycamore to Upper Sandusky, Ohio only a few miles away. The latter was my dad's hometown. I remember a lot about my life before that move. I had a friend, a monkey, an invisible friend named Zippy who was my friend prior to our move. He lingers in my thoughts to this day. We would "play" together all the time.

One of the really great memories I have of being young was when my grandpa would come to visit us from his home in West Virginia. He was my mom's dad. He had experienced more than one stroke so he walked slowly with a cane. He slept in my room and I remember hearing him sleep with labored breathing and snoring. I loved him and enjoyed being with him. We would walk around our big back yard, which was enclosed with a white picket fence. He was a nice man who was kind to me and just nice to be with. I did not meet my Grandma Sowards nor my Grandma and Grandpa Johnson; I have always wondered what they were like.

I especially remember that beautiful white picket fence and my mom's garden. It was big, and I was even called upon to do some important weeding and the picking of delicious vegetables from that garden. I remember having two dogs. One dog gave me fleas (I was allergic to them), so my dad sold the dog. The other dog was Fritz, a dachshund. Fritz dug his way out of our yard beneath our white picket fence, and that was it…, he was gone forever. I liked and still do like dogs, but mine have never stayed with me very long.

For whatever reason, I seem to remember a lot about the lives of my mom and dad. My mom came from a family of seven. When I was young, all of her siblings except my Aunt Ollie lived in West Virginia. We would go on vacation there each year, and some of them would reciprocate by coming to Ohio to visit. My dad's family was different in this regard. As I said, I never met my Grandfather and Grandmother Johnson. Dad's parents were deaf mutes; they could neither hear nor talk. My dad knew sign language and when we would go visit his relatives who were deaf, I would sit in the room watching and listening to their fingers move next to one another. I also anticipated the occasional laugh they would share. It was interesting to meet that side of the family; they were always very nice and really enjoyed the company that we delivered on our visits. My dad was an only child. Because his parents could not hear, he got away with a lot of things which ultimately got him in trouble. He was in his share of fights and counseled me to never back down. First, I want to share some about my dad; we will talk about mom later.

*****

There are a lot of good things I remember about my dad. He loved me, and I loved him, but, like anyone else, he had his faults. One of the most interesting events with my dad occurred when I was in the seventh grade. As I was seated in my home room, I was told to sit perfectly still as a corrective measure.

I had been goofing off, which was very typical for me. The seventh grade home room teacher laid my hands flat on my desk. He then informed me that every time I moved even a finger it would result in one swat with the "paddle," which was in the principal's office. You know I had seen that "paddle" and had heard about students having it applied vigorously to their backsides. It was never my intention to have an encounter with the "paddle" and have it be a part of the history of my junior high years. I moved my fingers seven times over a period of about twenty minutes and had to go to the principal's office. So here is the problem. Have you ever tried to lay your hands down flat on a desk and not move your fingers? I thought it was hard then and still do today. I was taken down to the office by this teacher and was greeted by the principal who had the "paddle" in his hand. He told me to lean on a desk next to the wall at which time he proceeded to give me seven whacks with the "paddle." The desk must not have been fully next to the wall because the first smack of the "paddle" moved the desk to the wall, Ouch…seven times.

When I arrived home that night my legs and backside were really red. I had welts all over. My parents took one look at my injuries and expressed their concerns. They talked to me and I told them the truth. It was my fault, but they determined the punishment was too severe for the crime. My dad lost control and took me down to that teacher's apartment and we had a talk. It turned out that this teacher had recommended me highly to the junior high football coach. Well, I had quit the team and this teacher thought he would punish me for quitting and embarrassing him. My dad was very angry, he had a terrific temper. He told the teacher that if he even so much as touched me again that he would come after him. My dad used language that I won't repeat here. He had his fists clenched and was ready to punch him out right then; I was scared and asked him not to hit my teacher. Dad cooled down, but that was one unforgettable night. By the way, my dad was very angry about my quitting the team, and we had a serious talk about quitting.

I believe that if we would have had the information when I was young that we do today about child development, ADD, ADHD, and anxiety that is currently available, my life may have been different. For sure, anxiety and fear were in my life, and I noticed them, but I thought they were just a natural part of life. I think my parents thought it was just a kid thing and there was nothing really wrong. However, that anxiety, fear, doubt, and even mild and intermittent depression became permanent fixtures in my life, to one degree or another. Anxiety and fear of what you may ask? I don't know! Failure? Embarrassment? Success?

Be assured, fear can become real in a person's life at a young age. I am sure that my mom and dad recognized stress, anxiety, fear, doubt and depression in themselves or other adults, but in a young child? I don't think they even gave it a thought. Why should they? We lived in a nice neighborhood, had good schools, plenty of food, nice clothes, and we loved one another. Today, the "Toxic Crew" is more noticeable in people of all ages.

Dad was a nice person and well liked in our town, but he did have a temper, was hypertensive, and his heart had been a concern for some time. He smoked at least a pack of cigarettes a day, and had done so for many years. There was potential for trouble in his life. I remember he and mom talking about these issues; she would encourage him to relax, not too smoke, and to lose that belly he had acquired.

*****

It was Monday February 25, 1963. I was twelve years old (would be turning thirteen in May), and we had moved from Sycamore to Upper Sandusky about seven years earlier. Over the weekend it had snowed, and on Monday there were a few inches of snow on the ground. There was, of course, snow on our sidewalks that needed to be shoveled. My dad told me to shovel the snow before I went to school. Guess what. I didn't do it. I put it off. I came home for lunch and had started to shovel the snow, but he came home and saw that I had not completed the job. He angrily took the shovel away from me and began shoveling the snow himself. He had just extinguished a cigarette. He had been directed by his doctor to quit smoking just days before this incident. This was not one of my dad's best moments. I went inside and awaited his arrival and the highly probable and most assuredly painful spanking I was going to reluctantly receive.

When he came in the house he was breathing heavily and was very much out of breath. He began scolding me and then stopped. He began to hold his chest and pace throughout the house. I had no idea what was going on, but my mom was fully aware of the situation. Her face told the story of her concern. She put her arms around him and tried to get him to relax and sit down. He could do neither, but finally the pain and the lack of oxygen caused him to lay down in the front room on the couch. He was no longer angry, he was scared. He knew he was in trouble. Everything was happening so fast that I could hardly comprehend what was going on, but I knew from what was being said, that dad was having a heart attack. He was just trying to stay calm so my sister and I would not be scared. It didn't work, by now we were both shaken by the events that were taking place.

He asked me to come to him as he lay on the couch. I did, and he said "Jimmy if anything happens to me you take care of your mom and sister..." I said I would and he told me and my sister Becky who was close by, that he loved us. My mom had called the ambulance. It was the local funeral home's combination hearse and ambulance which was common in the 1950's and early 1960's. My mom had called the doctor first, so he arrived before the ambulance. As all of this played out before our eyes, she asked the doctor if she could ride in the ambulance. I remember him saying no and I later found out he didn't think dad would make it to the hospital. One week later on March 4, 1963 at 4:45AM he died. He was forty eight years old and had suffered miserably for one week before his passing.

When the call came for my mom to go to the hospital that very early Monday morning, other family members were present. Her two sisters, her brother and an aunt had come to visit from West Virginia, knowing that dad was in a dreadful state. My mom's brother drove her to the hospital. Those left behind were weeping and praying. It wasn't long before my mom and uncle returned with the bad news. I remember it like it just happened; she walked to the doorway between the hallway and front room where I was sleeping on the couch. Leaning on the doorway she said "honey, daddy's gone." I just lay back down on the couch, covered my head with a pillow, cried and tried to figure it all out.

I am unable to describe how I felt at that time. I had some anger and of course a deep feeling of loss. The truth is I was just mixed up and I didn't do so well after his passing. In this world things happen that can blow you away. Even today what I read and hear daily about losses that people experience does make me think about the heartache they are experiencing.

Somehow though life goes on and you learn to live through it and move forward. Something was lost fifty years ago that simply could not be replaced by a human being. No one could ever replace him and no one ever tried. I did have a close relationship with an uncle who died two years after my dad's passing. There is a hope that is directly connected to my faith in Jesus Christ. I am very thankful that He lives forever and that I will see Him and other loved ones that have left our midst. That is Good News for anyone who has experienced loss in this life.

*****

I was an only child until I was nine; that is when my sister Rebecca was born. My mom was forty-five years old when she delivered Becky into this world. Her pregnancy was difficult; she had swollen ankles for months prior to going to the hospital and as I found out later, she was unsure if she would survive. She later explained that she had an out of body experience. The doctor's verified that she had died; she had no pulse for some time. All the while she was up toward the corner of the room looking down on her body and listening to the doctors express their grave concern about her condition. She said that just as quickly as she was out of her body, she returned and felt the pain that was associated with her experience at that moment.

*****

I enjoyed playing sports with my friends and especially with my dad. As I mentioned, he loved sports and I caught his enthusiasm and developed a passion for baseball. When he died all of that changed. I became disinterested in sports and many other important aspects of life.

Our family didn't seem to be overlooked when it came to sorrow. Over a six year period of time my mom and three of her sisters lost their husbands, my uncles. One of those uncles had become close to me but died in 1965, two years after my dad. I tell you, my world had changed and was going to continue to change.

*****

On New Years Eve of 1963, the year dad died, my four year old sister was in our upstairs bathroom. She attempted to clean up some bubble bath she had spilled on the floor. We had a small stove to keep the bathroom warm and in the process of cleaning she pushed the dust mop too close to the stove and we had fire. By the time I found out about it the flames were wrapping around the door jamb and were visible from the hallway. Mom told me to call the fire department while she proceeded upstairs to fight the fire…she extinguished most of it before the fire department arrived. She was exhausted and had breathed in a lot of smoke which for several weeks afterward negatively affected her breathing…but, she saved our house.

In addition to the obvious loss we had experienced as a family, we also lost our President John F. Kennedy to an assassin's bullets. As I write this I can feel the sadness of that time. I can also sense the strength we had as we hung tough together as a family.

FIRST PIECE OF MY LIFE PICKED UP
- A NEW DADDY -

The loss of my dad had to be the first real piece of my life that I experienced falling away. I am not sure why I didn't worry about my mom or dad dying, I just didn't. I know now that when a parent dies it really changes things, the daily things like looking for him to come home, playing ball with him or just talking to him. The death of a parent also exposes the loss that other family members are experiencing. A term that I use to describe the loss of a parent is "dark."

You see, even though it has been over fifty years since he died, I can still feel the emptiness and can even remember the smell of the flowers that were brought from the funeral home to our house after the funeral. How does a person replace a parent? I mention somewhere else in the book that you don't.

But, I do believe that pieces of one's life can be picked up. Just as we and our life situations change and we may not appear quite the same or act the same, a fallen piece of one's life may be different in some ways as well. When you pick it up it even looks different, but it restores and fills the emptiness that existed.

I missed the male influence of my dad most. When people tell me that a mom can fill the spot of a lost daddy, I know better, I have lived it. My mom is my hero, I loved her, still do and will never forget her, but she could never replace my dad.

So how can an important piece of life like this be picked up and restoration take place? After this loss I had years of heartache. Then, I made Jesus Christ Lord of my life, the love of the Father entered, restored and filled the empty places in my life. Serving Jesus Christ is a relationship not a religion. The love that the Lord showed me has permitted me to live more fully and with joy I never thought I could have.

He has given me the opportunity to be with my wife for fourty-four years. I watched as my dad was only able to share a part of that time with my mom. I have been blessed to be a daddy to three sons and be a part of my children's lives in everyday things as a Dad should. He showered me with the rewards of that experience, and now being a grandfather to two beautiful girls.

Though my life could have skidded totally out of control, Jesus Christ stepped in and led me to safety. I am sure my dad would have tried to help in that regard as well. There are so many things one can say about having a relationship with someone who can love you after the loss of a loved one.

Many (of you) look or have looked for a replacement daddy. Maybe you don't now or have never had your dad in your life; I have an answer for you. When one looks around and is unable to find that person that loves unconditionally, regardless of what has happened in your life, no matter what you have or have not done, let me recommend Jesus Christ, He loves unconditionally; His love, is called Grace.

This experience gave me hope and security that I hadn't had since I was a child when my dad and mom were both alive. I was brought into a new family, the family of God. In 1974, eleven years after my dad died, I picked up this piece of my life.

THINGS TO CONSIDER

So what's the point?

As I reflect on my life to this point I can see where anxiousness, fear, doubt and some depression were a part of my life when I was young. *We are all afraid at some time or other. But I know that there was a culture of fear that had developed in my life. It could have been from anything but you are able to see where I experienced it.* How about you?

What do anxiety and fear look like? They take many shapes and sizes…each time a challenge arises it can cause stress, make a person shudder, pull back, or not show up. After you do this for a while you begin to lose ground whether in everyday life, academics or relationships and it doesn't matter how old you are, anxiety and fear can negatively impact you. Remember; "The shadow of a dog never bit anyone." "Fear is: False Evidence Appearing Real? (Original author unknown.") What do stress, anxiety, fear and doubt look like to you? Think! Write a few notes.

_____
_____
_____
_____
_____
_____.

*****

What should we do when the impact of loss hits? We may feel like running, but we should take a deep breath and understand that the impact of loss usually lessens over time. We should not let it stop us from living out what we have been called to do in life. I believe my dad would have been disappointed in the way I responded to his death. He would have been surprised that I quit baseball. I believe he would have been remarkably surprised how many other important life things I quit. Most often to overcome loss it is literally putting one foot in front of the other, walking through and eventually out of it. Here is where faith in God is really relevant. (Heb.13:8.) "Jesus Christ the same yesterday and today and forever." He never changes, He is always there and if we can begin to have faith in Him, we will find that He will deliver. Sometimes He delivers differently than we expect but it is always better than anything we could have done on our own. (Isa.55:8) tells us that His thoughts and ways are higher than ours. It also says that His thoughts are higher than ours. I like having someone who can understand and see things perfectly, with precision and accuracy and is able to create the very best for me. That is Good News!

*****

I quit junior high football; I quit baseball when dad died. I would not show up at school to take a test, even though I had to take it sooner or later. I quit doing homework and would lie as to why; later in life I quit other things that ultimately impacted my life negatively. It happened to me and can happen to anyone. Out of control stress, anxiety and fear will keep you from participating in life as you should. Jesus said "...I am come that they may have life, and that they might have it more abundantly" (Jn. 10:10). I believe it, I have seen Him work. Do you feel like quitting, just giving up?

DON'T DO IT!

Anxiety and fear cause us to overcompensate...we may do things that are immature, or over reactions to certain situations. We then get embarrassed and fear causes us to run away and hide, again and again.

Have you ever found yourself overcompensating? Think! Write a few notes...

_____
_____
_____
_____
_____
_____
_____
_____
_____.

Solutions: We must realize that fear is a spirit and it is subject to us in Jesus Name. Use that Name! Speak it out loud at the enemy and the anxiety, fear and doubt that are messing with your life. There is nothing healthy about this fear which leads to more doubt and anxiety. Don't give into it. Refuse, absolutely refuse to participate in those treacherous and debilitating "games" that fear presents. People say that is not easy to do. I say it is when you identify it, and use your faith in Jesus to fight it off. This takes some effort, but the real work is being done by Christ. This is where faith comes into play. We must believe that as children of God we have power. "...because greater is he that is in you, than he that is in the world," (I Jn. 4:4).

Today and for many years I have experienced a real relationship with Jesus Christ, today I understand more about life with Him. Since I was converted in late 1974, the relationship I have had with my heavenly Father through Jesus Christ has been amazing. The beginning was incredible and to this day when I tell people about how this relationship started and what happened to me, they say that it is a rare experience. I could not disagree more! Millions and millions of people experience this supernatural experience. I have learned that no one can replace my earthly father with another earthly father; and no one can replace my relationship with Jesus Christ. He is the one who has stood in the gap for me many times; He is my all in all.

CHAPTER TWO

"CHANGE"

My world had changed, though the six years after we had moved were good, it seemed that things had just become more difficult and challenging. When dad died, a new world began. It wasn't all bad for sure, it was a time when I did go further off track, which took me where I didn't really want or need to go. One can blame lots of things on other people and circumstances, but I really believe that I was as much to blame as anyone or anything in regard to my circumstances. Then, as now, the one common denominator in my life is me. This may shock you, but the same is true for you…when you see this, you begin to look at life differently and for the good. Someone told me that this was and is a brilliant observation, a real awakening, and I agree it is important to understand this about ourselves.

My home town in Northwest Ohio was a nice place and it remains so to this day. The friends I had were basically no different than me; we were growing up and doing so in the volatile 60's. As I reflect on my life, I know that even then I was struggling for approval by others. I don't know why but I had a feeling of rejection by my peers. I know I said and did things just to get the attention of others. I acted foolishly for sure...it would have probably been called immaturity. Even though I did not act as I should, there were others around me struggling and they did other things to gain attention as well...but I was just being me and I think I often acted out of fear and anxiousness. I look back and see opportunities that I squandered just because of fear. Some of my friends were simply cooler than me and are probably still to this day. You know what? Now, right now, that's OK!

It was a weird time in which to live. Television was showing us things we had never seen before. It covered the Vietnam War almost in real time, close enough that we saw things that happened yesterday rather than a week ago. With the assassination of President Kennedy the same year my dad died and the fire in our house that year as well, I can tell you, my world was at the very least, being shaken. The President's Brother Robert Kennedy, Martin Luther King Jr., and Malcolm X were all assassinated in the 60's. John Glenn from Ohio was the first man to orbit the earth and Neil Armstrong also from Ohio was the first man to step on the Moon. An anti-war rally in northeast Ohio at Kent State University saw students shot and killed by the National Guard; all of this in the sixties and there were riots all over the country concerning the war in Vietnam. The drug culture was spreading into every nook and cranny of our society and alcohol which had been around thousands of years was being mass produced and distributed all over the country. Regretfully many young people and others during that time found out how addictive alcohol and drugs were. Many of us from that era found ourselves looking for the next drink or party instead of focusing on life, work, family or just being a normal teenager.

In March of 1963 when my dad passed I was not doing all that well in school. He didn't like that and neither did my mom because neither of them had finished high school. They wanted better for me and my sister. It all eventually turned out OK, but it took time, years and years. Anxiety and fear were major factors in my young life and at the time I did not realize it and neither did my parents. I mentioned that the incident with my dad and my home room teacher was one of the first times I actually recognized fear being present in my life. However, as I now recall and evaluate my life, I can see evidence of fear as early as elementary school. I was afraid to be in front of the class to present or do a math problem on the chalk board. I remember those times, not in general but in some instances very specifically.

*****

I remember the day not long after my dad died that my mom, sister and I walked uptown to the First Building and Loan and met with Paul who was the manager. Mom said she wanted to pay off the house in full. He told her that was not necessary. But she insisted and wrote the check from the insurance money we had received. That way she was sure that at least we would have a house that was ours. She was fearless and was able to see through the fog of mourning and grief and do what was best for our family.

Though we didn't give much thought to it at the time, my sister and I were in a single parent family and it was different for sure. I believe my mom's approach to being single and rearing two children was key to the ultimate successes that occurred for both my sister and me. She grew up during the great depression and for the most part lived in rural areas in southern Ohio and northern West Virginia. Her family moved some, but not a lot. She was one of seven children and had learned to share. In some regards she was extremely independent. She had grit and was not akin to losing; even though she had experienced failures in her life. When she focused on something it usually moved where she wanted it to move.

She refused to feel sorry for herself. She had pride in who she was. That personal pride helped her as she worked many long hours as a seamstress and tailor. Because she worked at home and her clients would come to the house to be fitted, she was at home a lot and worked long hours into the night when it was quiet. It was not unusual for her to work fifteen to twenty hours a day. She was very bright and as I recall, only completed the 8th grade. She loved to read and when it came to the welfare of Becky and me, I tell you she did not skim over the details; she was focused. What was the difference between my mom and many single mom's today? She had a made up mind, faith and to the extent she could, she trusted others around her who offered to help in some situations. There was no welfare subsidy…the only monies we received were the fruits of her labors.

Mom grew up in a time where having sex just to have sex was not the thing to do. Getting pregnant outside of marriage and or having a child outside of marriage were just not right. Her warnings to me and my sister in this regard were forthright. She did not look to the government for exceptional help, only that which had been promised through my dad's pension plan; he was a public employee at the time of his death. She was wise with her money. She didn't over eat and neither did we. We had selected TV shows which we were permitted to watch and then the TV was turned off. This changed as we moved into the late 60's and mom took a job outside of the house. She simply did not look to others to fulfill her needs. She worked hard and though not a church attender, she prayed with faith and hope and moved forward.

I do believe the sense that people are owed something just because they exist is of paramount importance to many in our country today. Buying things on credit when you can't afford to pay them off was out of the question for my mom. I don't remember not having the necessities of life and more. My actions were disappointing and I paid for those later in life. I did not get good grades in junior and senior high, but she hung in there, sacrificed and tried to get me the help I needed. She never gave up! We never had men roaming in and out of the house to be company for her. She loved and protected us, and that was so very important to our overall welfare. Though not a great church attender, she knew her Bible. She had some disagreements with some denominational teaching, but she never let that stand in the way of her faith in Jesus Christ. She believed that if she did her best for us and for herself, a loving God would step in the gap and meet our needs…she was right.

*****

In review, the 60's were challenging times. I no longer played baseball, I quit. My grades were not good and it not only seemed that my world was going the wrong direction, it was. I was making a fool of myself in more ways than one. My mom was brave and smart and with her hard work as a seamstress and then as a grocery store manager, she kept us financially sound. Though she felt inadequate to some in her family in regard to faith in God and did not go to church regularly, she believed in the Christian principles of faith she had been taught in her home and was rock solid as a Christian. She was great and my hero!

*****

I was blessed though I didn't realize it. When I was eleven my dad bought a power lawn mower. This was a big deal for our family. He was procured me the job mowing lawns for the department of water and sewer. He was a meter reader and when he found that they needed someone to mow, he bought the new mower and made sure I had the job. Work has always been an important part of my life.

A business owner, named Jim, owned several businesses including a SOHIO Gasoline Station took the recommendation of an employee (a friend of our family) and hired me to work part-time. I was thirteen, washed cars (25 cents a car), learned to pump gas and help with his other businesses (a soft water delivery service, septic tank service, U-Haul Rental business). I was constantly torn between wanting to participate in sports, other school activities and work…but I liked the money and frankly, I learned a lot at work.

When I was thirteen while working at the station I was checking the oil in a customer's car that had stopped to get gasoline. We always checked the oil, radiator, the air filter and belts. On this hot day I was checking the fluids on the car and even though it was hot outside and the engine was hot, I felt it was OK to try and check the radiator water level. I had no more than touched the radiator cap than it blew off and hot anti-freeze filled water sprayed into my face. I ran into the garage bay and with my friend's help I washed my face and eyes with cool water. I was then taken by car to the local hospital.

Mom was at home and on the phone with my Aunt Ollie when the operator interrupted their call to tell mom about me. She was given instructions to go to the hospital where I had been taken for care. I am sure she wondered what would happen next. Life was just full of the unexpected for our family. It all turned out OK, mostly second degree burns but it sure did hurt for a while. Depending on the person's make up, when a series of mostly negative events occur it is not unusual for stress leading to anxiety, fear and doubt to arise. Sometimes expectations concerning life change as well.

The owner of Jim's SOHIO was very nice and always treated me fairly. He worked hard and expected us to do the same. I began to work a few more hours and began earning 50 cents an hour; I was happy. Working kept me out of trouble but I was influenced by some older boys…they knew more about life than I did and so I received a basic education about life. As I look back, it was probably too much information.

Each Saturday at the gas station there was a man who would pull in, we would fill his car with gas and he would drive to the side of the station, come inside and pay for his gas. Those were not the days of self serve. While he was inside, he would give us some instructions about washing and servicing a car that a friend would be bringing in shortly.

He would wait in his car until his lady friend would pull in and park her car. He would get out, open the door for her and they would drive away for the day. They arrived at almost the exact time each Saturday and left that evening at almost the exact same time as well.

I was the one who usually washed the car. This man always gave a nice tip for having the car washed and serviced and for all of us to keep our mouths shut about this meeting of two "friends." Interestingly I made 25 cents for washing the car and was required to do an extra good job. Anyway, when the gentleman returned in the evening with his lady friend, she would go directly to her clean car and he would come inside and pay. He gave a $3.00 tip. So, whoever was able to receive his payment had power over the tip. If I checked him out, I had to give my friend at least one dollar of the $3.00 sometimes more. But if I could somehow take his payment and no one else was around I would keep it all for myself. If my friend would take the payment I would only get 50 cents…not a great deal of fairness in all of that, but 50 cents was a big deal at that point in my life.

Once I decided to sneak (steal) some money from the cash register to go to the county fair. This was a stupid move but I took the money and convinced myself I was cool. Then one of the older guys that worked with me noticed I was on a spending spree. He reported me to Jim and when he was done with me I had learned my lesson. There wasn't any political correctness about his approach to me…I was a thief. He physically threw me the best part across the room against a wall. As I slid down the wall and sat on the floor he then threatened me with the loss of my job and going to jail; I did get the message. If my dad would have been around he would have given me another beating. I learned and went on to work for Jim for a while longer until a better job came up and I moved on. I owe a lot to Jim in more ways than one. After all of these years, I wish I could share with his family how important he was to me.

Our neighbor was the county treasurer and during my teenage years helped me procure employment in the county engineer's office. I worked on a survey crew which was a good job for a teen. It was a summer job and I earned a good income.

The neat thing about it was that over the next few years when I needed some work, even when I was out of school, they accommodated me. It was a blessing; I viewed it as merely a job, but it was much more than that.

Today, I reflect on all of the young boys that are growing up without a loving dad. Our society is in a mess in regard to political correctness and the virtual purging of young men from the workplace, because often it doesn't pay employers to hire high school students. This reality is disconcerting to me.

When I was young, there was an expressed sense of right and wrong that was pervasive in the community. It was built on the teachings that people had received from those who shared biblical principles about respect, the value of life, working for what you get, a certain respect for authority and on and on.

I was no angel and very confused, yet the basic underpinnings of life were embedded deep within me. Later on when my life was about to whirl out of control, something inside said no and I took a different direction. I am thankful for the input from my elders of which many were not family members.

Anxiety and fear can influence a life at any age, but fear and anxiousness when one is young can set the stage for a catastrophic future. Here is the deal; often times when people are fearful and anxious it can be interpreted as something else. Maybe our self esteem needs to be improved? Maybe we are just shy? Today children are misdiagnosed with ADD and ADHD when anxiety is the problem. We, who are fearful because of life experiences that have shaped us, may find we have to deal with an addiction, joblessness, inability to complete our education, stay married or a dozen other things. Anxiety and fear just keep on giving or should I say taking.

THINGS TO CONSIDER

When I think about anxiety, the first thing I think about is fear, doubt runs a close second and then depression follows. Can you recall when you were anxious and fear raised its ugly head and you began to doubt? My mom overcame fear and doubt to take money of which she didn't have much and pay off the house.

How about you, can you relate a story when you were anxious and fear became a big player? Did you overcome it or did it overcome you? Think and write a few notes.

_____
_____
_____
_____
_____.

Have you noticed the blessings in your life? When I was young I didn't see the blessings. People blessed me with work, correction and hope, I didn't get it. On reflection were you ever blessed by others and didn't realize it? Why didn't you see it? I think I missed watching God work for me in so many ways and I really didn't recognize it was Him, I thought I was lucky. How about you? Are you more thankful and do you have a spirit of gratitude for the good things that have and are happening to you? Do you consider lessons learned as blessings? Think! Write a few notes…

_____
_____
_____
_____
_____.

Does a positive, moral, value system make a difference in your life? I noted that my mom's generation was different than ours. Even though there were plenty of people who did wrong and always will, my mom being a decent woman and not bringing men in or going out to meet men was important to our family. When you reflect on the situations we have today with so many families crushed by wrongdoing, so many children without their father in their home and lives, when you reflect on those who simply make a mess of everything because of a different value system, which value system do you feel is most important and why? Think! Write a few notes...

_____
_____
_____
_____
_____
_____
_____.

Don't you think a good value system makes life better? Think! Write a few notes.

_____
_____
_____
_____
_____
_____
_____.

Change really does change things doesn't it? In your life, my life and the lives of those we love, our neighbors and fiends? How do you handle change? How do you think you should handle change? Does including God in the equation sound good to you? Do you know how to include Him? Think! Write a few notes

_____
_____
_____
_____
_____.

Remember my Saturday car wash experience and the inequity that usually occurred? Remember, if I could position myself just right I could get more of the money? Truth: I deserved more. I worked hard. How do you handle inequity? Are you entitled? Do you have a method of working through things when they don't go your way? Think! Write down a thought or two on this. Is your answer one of thanks for what you have or of displeasure because of what you can't have? Think! Write a few notes.

_____
_____
_____
_____
_____
_____.

CHAPTER THREE

"MY TEENAGE CHALLENGE"

I was learning a lot as a young teenager. It was a Thursday night, Thanksgiving evening 1965 I wanted to go to a party in the evening; my mom approved and gave me a midnight curfew.

There was beer at this party and of course I drank too much; I was seriously drunk. I was so drunk I was unable to walk home, so these two guys I knew said they would take me. As I recall they became side-tracked which meant we drove around and drank some more with me in the car. I recall that we didn't stay in town but drove out of town into the country to a bar and carry out where they purchased more beer using fake I.D.'s I ended up at home before 12:00 midnight. I was drunk when I walked in and yelled to mom that I was home; and immediately went upstairs and slept until noon the next day.

My dad liked a beer once in a while. My mom would have a taste and walk away; we didn't have much around the house at any one time. There were times when dad and I would walk uptown to Pete's Carry Out. On a hot summer night there would be some guys he knew hanging out, enjoying a cold drink. I would have a soft drink and he would have a cold beer, sometimes two. Even though he drank a lot before he was married, he settled down quite nicely in that regard. However, each Christmas Eve he would come in "tipsy." He was a part-time bartender at the Elks Club, but he never appeared to me to be careless with drinking.

After my Thanksgiving beer drinking experience, my life began to gradually spiral out of control. I was never arrested for drunk driving or under aged drinking but in that school year 1965-66 things were getting noticeably out of control. I was on the football, basketball and track teams as a student trainer. I didn't have to maintain good grades to be on the team in that position. As I look back, I can see where the coaches kept me in the game of life by letting me be a part of their teams. Interestingly I did some really cool things as a student trainer that had colleges and universities interested in me attending their schools, but that is a story for later.

I wanted to stay active in sports and the permission to do so in this manner probably kept me from a lot of trouble. However, there was plenty of trouble in regards to failing subjects and getting involved with some older guys and even some girls. It was a challenging time for me on the emotional front as well as academically. During this time mom paid plenty of attention to me, correcting and grounding me as needed. She really was up against it as a single mom taking care of two kids. As I look back, I see more clearly how she maneuvered as a parent so as not to run me off. She worked diligently at keeping control of her family.

James W. Johnson Ph.D.

*****

I told you that I did poorly in school and so bad that I had to go an extra year to graduate. Twice during high school my mom at my request sent me to military school, and both times I returned with better study habits. The first time I attended was in the fall of 1966. At the time, military and other private schools would advertise in the back of popular magazines such as Redbook, Family Circle and others. I recall mom threatening to send me to military school if I was not good and did not improve my grades. I would look in the back of her magazines at those schools to learn more about them. It all looked good to me, but I don't think I was realistic about such things. Military school meant a disciplined life, no drinking, not sitting alone in my room reading hot rod or sporting magazines. I did sense that I needed help and soon became familiar with one particular military school, from which I requested information. I dreamt of being there, in my uniform and how I would show people how cool I was and would come back home during the holidays in my uniform and impress everyone. These schools cost a lot of money which we did not have a lot of. She saved and saved just to keep things going.

So in the summer of 1966 I began to prepare for military school. I had purchased a two tone turquoise and white 1957 Chevrolet with the money I had saved from mowing lawns and other work. Because I wanted to go to military school I was willing to sell the car just a couple of months after buying it. This was a BIG DEAL! I had failed three subjects that past year and had to make up an English course during the summer. From an academic perspective I believe this is where out of control stress manifested into noticeable anxiety, fear and doubt. I had faced many challenges in math early on in my education, and during my sophomore year those challenges were more than obvious.

During that summer I was working for mom's cousin Roy. He owned a car dealership at which I would wash cars and could use the garage to work on my 1957 Chevy. Incredibly, in the midst of everything during that busy summer I also contracted mononucleosis. I was so sick that I was in the hospital for several days. I really wondered what else was going to happen to me. I was afraid of losing my job, failing my summer English course and right then we had decided that I would go to Military school in Georgia...what would happen next?

According to our plan, we sold the car, I finished the summer English course and somehow though still recovering from being sick, the military school approved my admittance. I had quit so many things I wonder yet today how she had the courage to take another risk with me. After all she did have to take care of my sister, our house and all that goes along with living. The school worked out a payment plan with her so I could attend.

As I recall, I boarded a Greyhound Bus to Georgia one summer night in August of 1966 and spent thirty-three hours on buses going down through Ohio, West Virginia, Virginia, the Carolinas, and finally into Northern Georgia. I remember waking up while the bus was traveling deep in the mountains of West Virginia and saw only rocks and trees; I had forgotten where I was and tried to get my bearings. During that time the Vietnam War was in full swing. The bus I was riding had a lot of military personnel aboard. I remember in the dimly lit bus at night, listening to soldiers singing. It was a sad and lonely time for many people. When I arrived in northern Georgia I was glad to get off of that bus. I went to the nearest pay phone, called mom collect and heard the relief in her voice as she heard her sixteen year old son's voice telling her all was well. I stayed overnight in a motel and awakened the next morning to catch a cab and travel to Riverside Military Academy. I arrived, signed in, picked up my uniforms, laundry bag, coat, hats, brass and all of the directions and instructions that go with being a new cadet. After lunch at my new school and a time of orientation, we practiced marching and learning basic formations.

This is a good a time to discuss how out of control stress, anxiousness, fear, doubt and depression the "Toxic Crew" mitigated my efforts. This should have been an exciting time for me and my family. Even though I was tired from being sick and needed extra rest, I should have been excited and engaged in trying to do my best. It was as though I wanted to do that, but inside I just couldn't. I was disinterested, lacked motivation to participate in classes, sports activities, whatever. I ended up in the infirmary numerous times; I missed having my pictures taken (in my dress uniform) and never did achieved the goals that were set for me. I came home late in the autumn of that year, I had quit again. It was as though I was afraid of success. As I write this I am embarrassed; fear and failure had become a permanent part of my life. People say to me, you just don't understand what it means to be down…you don't know what it means to be depressed etc., yes I do and when I reflect on my past, I can see how it negatively impacted my life and that of my family. By the way, when I returned home everyone made excuses for me, oh he was sick etc. The truth is that I was gripped by fear and doubt…I don't believe I was able to see myself as successful at a high level. If I was called upon in class I would freeze. Even if I had the answer, I forgot it. Nonetheless, I began to do better in school. My time in military school had not been a complete loss.

As I arrived on campus I was both young and a poor student. It didn't take long for me to become homesick. Interestingly, my roommate was David Duke who later became the Grand Wizard of the Ku Klux Klan and a candidate for President. Remember, I was only there from August to November of 1966. David Duke was OK as a roommate and I was able to learn from our discussions. He was unabashedly anti-Semitic and I had been taught that the Jewish people were God's chosen. He was very protective of his race and though I did not grow up in a racially integrated area, I was always taught to respect all people regardless of the color of their skin. David was so outspoken in opposition to what I had been taught in this regard that I was often shocked by his comments. There were several things I found interesting about David, and the one thing that seemed to really occupy his thoughts, was listening to the news. In those days we did not have television in our rooms; it was spartan to say the least. We were, however, permitted to listen to the news on the radio at the top of the hour, when we were in our room. Whenever David had the opportunity to listen he did and he would always comment on what he had heard. I was sixteen and being made aware of things I had never heard of before. His view of the news was totally different than mine. He would mention world leaders that I viewed as enemies to freedom, but to David they were to be respected. David did not change my mind in the short time we roomed together. He became a very public figure and I have not been surprised by what I have read and heard of him since that time. Though we were different, David and I always got along.

In 1988 David Duke sought to be on the ballot in Michigan for President of the United States. The Michigan Republican State Committee (MRSC) met to vote to approve or disapprove his name being on the ballot. I was very involved in politics in

Michigan at that time and a close friend of mine was on the MRSC. The evening of that vote this friend became aware that a member of the committee was going to be absent. I was asked to be a proxy and vote in the absent member's place. How ironic that I had the opportunity to vote on whether David would be on the ballot for President as a Republican in Michigan. I am sure David was never aware of the unusual situation I was in that night.

*****

My study habits improved and I was a student trainer for the basketball and track teams that year. I did find an interest in American History and did quite well in that class and related classes. I was back home and the old habit of drinking, when I could without getting caught was back as well. However, in the summer of 1968 I returned to military school to take Algebra. It was a bit less formal than the regular school year, as we wore our uniforms, but without ties. The summer was hot in northern Georgia. I did OK that summer and came home having some success. I even overcame a knee injury…quite an accomplishment for me.

I mentioned earlier that I had a knee injury. It bothered me occasionally and I will tell you now that fear and a minor injury almost caused me to fail again and not have a successful summer. I forget now how it occurred, but I injured my knee in one of my sports activities. I had some swelling and pain etc. Anxiety and fear rose up and I began to make a big deal out of what was a minor knee injury. I was on crutches and it wasn't long before I was on a flight back to Ohio to see my doctor. After I saw some of my friends and went to one of our watering holes; I returned to military school to finish the summer semester. I came back home at the end of the summer with some success and for the most part overcoming the "Toxic Crew." That was one of the few times I had won that battle…it felt good, really good.

I then went into my senior year as a student trainer and the truth is I really did much better. I seemed to be more confident and experienced a degree of success, of which I was unaccustomed. In addition, I wrote for the sports section of our daily newspaper covering midget football and did well at this. However, to catch up after all of the poor academic work of the past was just too much. I learned a great lesson about working hard and keeping up. Falling behind and trying to catch up is really tough especially when the things before you, the new challenges, are even greater.

Overall, I did really well my senior year. I was also recognized for all of my hard work through high school as a student trainer when I received an invitation from the head trainer at Denison University to attend a National Athletic Trainers Association (NATA) Clinic and the Dennison Relays at which we would work with the college athletes. I enjoyed athletics, participating in physical fitness activities and even created a circuit training program. I was engaged in related study and making an effort to improve my personal strength. My efforts in this regard even spread to the coaches. Remember, I was a high school student in my 5th year of high school with average grades. The question is, could I overcome the fear and doubt that always beset me and make something of myself?

In the spring of 1969 I was accepted at The Ohio State University on a probationary basis. This was not the best way to start college for sure. Though I stopped playing competitive sports, except for intramural, I always found myself wanting to be involved. So over the course of five years of high school, I earned 11 varsity letters as a student trainer. Though I chose to attend Ohio State, I had several MAC and two Big Ten schools interested in me as well.

*****

How did I get to Ohio State? When I was in my junior year my knee was giving me trouble. I had tried out for Varsity Basketball and had reinjured it. I thought I should try-out, I did and I was OK with my effort. I was referred by my friend, mentor and our team physician to a group of orthopedic surgeons in Columbus. The surgeon who met with me was named Judson D. Wilson. At that time I had no idea that he was a truly gifted surgeon and had been honored for his service in WWII. Regardless, after he looked at my knee he said I should have surgery. We worked through that, and set the date. We then discussed OSU athletics; we were both" fans." He then informed me that he was a team physician for the Buckeyes and as we talked about my student training involvement at the high school level, he did something very special for me. He asked me if I would be interested in coming to OSU. I hesitantly said yes, because I knew what Dr. Wilson didn't; I was not prepared to do college work. He reached over and picked up his prescription pad, tore off a sheet and wrote a note. It was a referral for me to meet Ernie Biggs the Head Trainer at OSU. I was to do so at the North Athletic Facility and do it right then, on my way home.

I did as he instructed. I walked into the facility and saw some of the biggest guys I had ever seen in my life…OSU football players. I asked to see Ernie and the rest was history. He liked me and to have a referral from one of the team physicians sealed the deal. I stopped by the university several times before I was out of high school and each time Ernie invited me in and talked for a while. Then in the spring of 1969 he formally invited me to The Ohio State University to be a student trainer. Success was before me. He included a financial grant and aid package as a part of the invite.

I was not prepared for college. I attended summer school at OSU but did poorly. Along with poor academics, I spent a lot of time on High Street and drank more than I should have. I began summer football practices at Ohio State as a student trainer on the freshman team and within a week I was working with the varsity players, the defending national champions. I was good at this and my instincts to detect injuries and help the players when injured was a special gift. I would come in early in the morning to start the whirlpools and to get things ready for the two a day practices. Interestingly, I continued to drink too much, but I was able to be at practices early in the morning, so there were no complaints.

I saw Coach Woody Hayes daily and worked with some of the best college football players in the country. I was at OSU and with the team until right before the first game when I quit. I just picked up and left, never told Ernie, just left, fear had overcome me again. I was selfish and considered no one but myself; not mom, Becky, or Dr. Wilson, no one. I tried to stay in school by attending the branch of OSU about 20 miles from my house, but I was disinterested and left. This is what the "Toxic Crew" can do if permitted to go unchecked.

It was gone; a college education and what I had hoped would be a career as an athletic trainer. What would make a person leave this opportunity? It was a big deal...couldn't I just stay and finish? I was afraid. Don't ask why or how, I was simply afraid; out of control stress led to anxiety and fear had gripped me again.

I remember the feeling, because I had it many times following that event, I felt pinned in, like I couldn't escape. Nobody was holding me back, or confining me, I just felt like I needed to escape. If somebody wasn't kind to me I wanted to leave rather than stand my ground. This is not a part of my life any longer but in the past it was a big deal.

*****

No longer in school, I was working and going to a nightclub regularly. On the night of the Ohio State – Michigan game in 1969 I had my first date with the young woman who became my wife. I am pleased the way things worked out in this regard and I am pleased to say we have been married for over forty three years as I write these words. Though not successful in college early on and setting aside a potentially wonderful career, I came out a winner. Mary and I were married a year later and the story gets very interesting from that point on.

THINGS TO CONSIDER

Have you ever hidden or are you right now hiding behind a mask? Maybe it isn't really you that people are seeing? Why? Don't you like who you really are? I didn't, my alcoholism was a mask. Each mask makes its own impact. Some who find their vocation in the fields of psychology, psychiatry and psychotherapy believe that alcoholism and other addictions as well as psycho-pathologies are long term. They may even believe they are forever, a way of life or continuum of existence; unless a medication can mitigate their ravaging symptoms. For some that may be true. I found that He is the one who strengthens me and in whom I am complete (Col. 2:10). Where are you today? Any mask that you would like to remove? How will you go about that? Will it include the awesome POWER of God? Think! Write a few notes...

_____
_____
_____
_____
_____
_____
_____
_____
_____
_____
_____
_____
_____
_____.

Addictions often come on slowly...be aware. Are you concerned about anything that you may be letting take too much of your time, talent, treasure? Think! Write a few notes...

_____
_____
_____
_____
_____
_____
_____.

I can tell you that anxiety and fear can change you. It can make you withdraw as it did for me in military school and at Ohio State. Is this or has this gone on in your life or the life of a loved one? Think! What can you do to help yourself or your loved one? Think! Write a few notes.

_____
_____
_____
_____
_____
_____
_____.

I know that getting behind whether in my personal life or in school or at work really impacted me. Getting behind academically really set the stage for me not getting ahead for years. Just as G.P.A's are really tough to raise so are other things in life. My recommendation is don't get behind. But, what happens when you do? Do you have the courage and strength to get back in the game? I think this is a good lesson to learn. Stay with things. Work hard be consistent and know that your actions now will influence your future. Think! Write a few notes...

_____
_____
_____
_____
_____
_____
_____
_____
_____.

CHAPTER FOUR

"SIGNING UP AND ALMOST SIGNING OUT"

Mary and I dated from late November 1969 through 1970 during which time we were engaged on March 19 and were married on December 19 of 1970. On December 1, 1969 during the draft lottery, a combination of my birth date and first letters of my first, middle and last names, qualified me to be inducted number forty-one. That meant I was going into the military very soon and probably to Vietnam. Soon thereafter I went to the draft board and made arrangements to take my physical and other exams to go into military service. During the physical they noticed the knee problems I had and they found a problem with my colon. None of this was serious enough to prevent me from being inducted. In September 1970, I took advantage of the opportunity to enlist in the United States Army Reserve. When Mary and I were married I had not yet been to basic training. I was attending meetings but active duty was still before me. I took the oath and I was in the Army. I was proud to be in the U.S. Army Reserve. I had been stressed and thus full of fear and anxiety about military service though I wanted to serve. As a member of the reserves I had more peace and felt things were finally moving forward on this front.

My dad and several of my family members served in the Army in WWII. The uncle that I had become close to and had passed away in 1965 had been in the Battle of the Bulge. I had a neighbor who had been a U.S. Marine and been in the Bataan Death March. I knew veterans of WWI who lived in our town and were suffering the results of encounters with mustard gas. My hometown had lost several young men in Vietnam and I had many friends who were there. I was no stranger to being around vets and hearing about war. Nonetheless I was only in the U.S Army Reserve for about four and one-half months when we were in an automobile accident that changed everything. From that point on because of the injuries incurred in the accident my date to go on active duty was delayed.

On January 17, 1971 on the way from Ohio to Detroit for the baptism of a niece, we were in a terrible auto accident near Wyandotte Michigan. We had been married one month when the accident occurred. We were both injured but Mary more seriously with two broken legs and other injuries. The following May, Mary gave birth to twin boys, Aaron James who was stillborn and our son Eric William who lived for 8.5 years.

There were six of us in the car including Mary's dad who was driving; her mom and two of her sisters. It was of course winter and it had recently snowed. That day two of the lanes were pretty clear going both north and south on I-75 north of Toledo and south of Detroit. Mary's dad was a good and careful driver – a wise man as well I might add. As we traveled north we were near Wyandotte Michigan and had just stopped to clean off the windshield. Mary's mom wanted to move to the back seat so Mary and I moved up to the front. Mary sat between her dad and me. We weren't using our seat belts that day though available, that was a common practice for many travelers at that time.

We had only been driving a short time when a young man who was southbound on I-75 at a high rate of speed for the conditions lost control of his car, came across two lanes of highway, the median, and hit us. We actually collided with the rear of his car which caused a fire. Dad had time to apply the brakes before the impact, and I remember Mary's sister yelling, "daddy look out, a car," but he couldn't avoid the collision, it was jarring. Mary was seriously injured, in and out of consciousness for over 11 days. She had two broken legs and an injured hand as well as bruised and cut up. Mary's two sisters were injured one with a badly broken leg. Mary's dad was beat up, with a cracked sternum, fractured ribs and other injuries. Mary's mom's face hit the back of my head in the collision. She received serious injuries to her face and jaw as well as having a broken leg.

Mary's dad was a strong man and even with his injuries he had the power to push with great strength and together we broke the seat so we could get out. I remember him saying "push Jimmy" as we began to push on the dashboard our adrenalin was enabling us, and that was the last thing I remember. The next thing I knew I woke up out on the highway between fire hoses and immediately looked for Mary. She wasn't far away but she was unconscious. I yelled and yelled at her and she finally awakened enough so that I knew she wasn't dead. I remember bits and pieces of things until we arrived at the hospital. The young man who hit us sat beside me in the front seat of the ambulance. Mary was in the back, but I don't recall who else was there with us.

I remember walking into the hospital. I had several fractured ribs some in front, others in the lower back area. I had a substantial cut in the back of my head from mom and me colliding. I walked around the emergency room looking at our family. Mary's youngest sister wasn't injured seriously; she was sleeping when the collision occurred, but everyone else was beat up. I walked around and was aware of what was going on and then they told me to lay down on a gurney, and that was it. I became so stiff and achy right away it was unimaginable, I hurt all over in just a few minutes. I was able to answer questions and I know dad was conscious as I heard him talking. I believe Mary's sisters were as well, but Mary was unconscious and mom was intermittently awake, but having trouble talking because of her injuries.

I was not in a private room or a semi-private room, but a ward. I was by far the youngest person in the room at twenty years of age. Newly married and here I was in this hospital room with other men that I did not know. Each had his unique physical situation or problem. Who would have ever believed I would be in this position? Each day as my condition improved I began to converse with men in the ward. I remember one man who was often belching and throwing up, but the others were quietly living through their condition. The overall conditions were good; as the room was clean and the staff polite and attentive to our needs.

As I walked around and spoke with some of the others I struck up a conversation with a man that I later found out was a Methodist Minister. He was nice and in considerable pain. As we talked one day he began to share Christ and the Gospel with me. I didn't want to hear about Christ and the Gospel. I was anxious to take Mary, get out of the hospital and get back to living a more normal life, which meant being together in our own apartment. I was also anxious to have a drink when I wanted one. Nonetheless, he was able to get my attention. He finished talking and gave me a paperback version of the Living Bible and told me I needed Jesus Christ in my life. He was correct, absolutely correct! I was not ready, but he had been a witness for Christ and that made a difference. I took that Bible and kept it for many years until I gave it to a thrift store for them to sell. I will never forget him. Even though I did not want to admit it then, I wanted more out of life than what I had and he was right, I needed Jesus Christ.

As I recovered from the auto accident, I kept my U.S. Army Reserve Unit updated on our situation. Mary was in a wheelchair with two broken legs as well as being pregnant and I was her primary caretaker. However, there was a major conflict going on in Vietnam and my unit needed to get me into basic training. I understood, but my world was still crazy and I did not want to leave Mary. The out of control stress occurring from the results of the accident, only fed anxiety and fear. All of this was similar to having gasoline thrown on a blazing fire. No excuses, it was just a fact, and I did not recognize it for what it was…the "Toxic Crew" was at work.

While I am telling you about the Methodist Minister in the hospital, I don't want to forget the story my mom shared with me after the accident. We were married at St. Michaels Roman Catholic Church in Findlay Ohio on December 19, 1970. My uncle Ernest who was a Pentecostal Preacher joined a Roman Catholic Priest and they presided over our wedding ceremony. My life was noticeably not committed to Christ and Mary agrees that she was a lukewarm Roman Catholic. Mary and I participated in pre-marital instruction as required by Mary's church. I didn't do well with the instruction and the priest who was teaching finally gave up; he did so primarily because of my terrible attitude. So when it came to the wedding day, both my uncle and the priest were going to participate; one giving me my vows and the other giving Mary hers. As the moment came for us to receive our vows my uncle stood up and gave us our vows. He and the priest had a discussion and this is how they resolved the issue.

So we were married and had a wonderful reception. As Mary and I were driving away, my uncle stood beside my mom and told her that Mary and I were going to be in an accident and we would be in a blue car. The car we drove away in was blue and my mom was terrified. He assured her it was a different blue car and though I would be injured I would be fine. He was right; the car we were in when the accident occurred was blue. Another God Thing!

There are many good things that have happened to me in my life. I don't want to leave the impression that everything was bad, it wasn't, but we had our challenges. Mary had been through the accident, hospitalization, two major surgeries and was confined to a wheelchair for months. Let me just say that Mary was incredible through all of this. She may have flinched a few times and even cried to herself…because it was tough on her for five months for sure, but she was brave and steadfast. I am not sure I really appreciated then what she was going through. As a twenty year old I was often caught up in the fact that I was her primary caretaker, with many every day duties and personal things to attend to. But upon reflection I can tell you the magnitude of what she went through was much greater than anything I was doing to help her.

*****

On April 30, 1971 Mary began to have labor pains. We weren't sure, but we thought that she was ready to give birth to our first child. The doctor made some effort to stop the labor but it was unsuccessful. As I recall, she went into the hospital late in the afternoon on April 30, she had a cast on one leg; and early in the morning of May 1, 1971 she gave birth to not one but two babies. Eric William Johnson was born at 3lbs.11ozs; however the other baby Aaron James was stillborn. I must tell you at age 20 I had no idea what was going on. At that time fathers weren't permitted to be in the delivery room. It was truly amazing…she was amazing. Knowing what I know today I can see just how special her courage and composure were. Eric would spend the next several weeks in the hospital as a low weight baby with some breathing and other challenges. Treatments were much different then, than today.

The U.S. Army Reserve was knocking on the door for me to go on active duty and here I was now, with not only an injured wife, but with a child. The Army had to do what they had to do and our situation appeared to be a mess. Here is where out of control stress leading to anxiety and fear become huge factors. I was anxious and my mind seemed to be whirling. I was unable to effectively make decisions. At times I was confused and had paralyzing fear. I had trouble prioritizing things that needed to be done and further more I had very little confidence in myself to make the right decisions. Does this mean I didn't make decisions? No, it was just a lot of work to think through the decision making process. In reflection, I can see that my alcohol consumption just added to the confusion. Nonetheless, Mary and I did successfully make important decisions.

As we moved on with our lives we began to see that Eric was not "normal." I remember one day Mary's mom and dad came over to our apartment. They had seven children of which

Mary was the middle child. As they watched him they saw things we didn't in regard to child development. Eric cried much of the time both day and night. When we visited the pediatrician, we began to find that things were not going well with Eric. I remember when we heard the diagnosis of Cerebral Palsy. Certainly Eric had been injured while in the womb at the time of the accident. Regardless, we began to travel that unique road that parents follow when they have a child that is both mentally and physically disabled. It was scary and of course we were simply unsure what Cerebral Palsy meant. We learned a lot! I tried to be a good husband and daddy but I was so immature and the alcohol was impacting me negatively. Alcohol was on my mind all the time. As I reflect on those days, the alcohol took the edge off of tense situations, but caused me to say and do things that only added to the frustration of living.

THINGS TO CONSIDER

I don't know where you are in your life. I don't know if you and I have yet to connect on life experiences. Maybe you can identify with me at some level, maybe not. I know that this period of my life was challenging.

Have you had a time in your life that was difficult, what did you do? Was it an unexpected pregnancy or an unexpected near tragedy or an unexpected illness? What has happened in your life that you had to adjust to?

Did you adjust well? Did your actions make things worse? This time of my life was really mixed up? Have you experienced that? Experiencing it now? Are you or a loved one in the middle of a mess? How do you adjust? If you haven't had an experience(s) that you had to adjust to what would you do if you had an unexpected situation? Think! Did you learn anything from the way I handled things or more important the way I didn't handle things? Think! Write a few notes…

_____
_____
_____
_____
_____
_____
_____
_____
_____
_____
_____
_____.

CHAPTER FIVE

"TRUSTING & MOVING"

So, as we went through the time of May, June, July into September, the pressure to go on active duty became intense. All totaled I think there were three orders issued for me to go to basic training; one was to Fort Leonardwood KS, another to Fort Knox KY, and yet another to Fort Dix NJ. All of these orders had been rescinded awaiting my full recovery from the accident as well as my family situation. I don't recall the exact date but I had gone on a weekend drill. It was an overnight bivouac and I recall that I felt odd leaving Mary and Eric overnight. I arrived at our Army Reserve Unit on Saturday morning. We drilled all day and then prepared to go out overnight and return Sunday. This is not that big a deal, but everything was a big deal to me right then. Mary's parents and my mom assured me all would be all right. But I was nervous, fearful and feeling inept as a husband, dad and now a soldier.

It was raining that day and as a part of a transportation unit we did some driving out in the community and returned to HQ close to evening. There was a 2nd Lt. who had been in Vietnam that had given me the oath, who was not pleased with me. By not being able to go on active duty I had become a real problem for him. He had given me a rough time that day and even embarrassed me by calling me names in front of the other guys. He was a good guy and in my eyes a hero, but he was also my worst enemy right then. He could hardly wait to get me on bivouac.

Late in the afternoon an officer came to talk with me privately. He treated me with respect and knew I was going to be in trouble if things didn't change. I either went on active duty or I was going to be punished. He and I had a talk that I will never forget. He told me he wanted to help me and my family and he thought what my family was going through was prohibiting me from being the kind of soldier I needed and wanted to be. He demonstrated confidence that I could do well in the military, but not in the condition I was in at that time.

I couldn't find my bearings. For example, if I had a compass and wanted to go due North I had trouble believing the compass when it was pointing due North. I didn't trust people as I should. If I felt strongly that I should do or say something, that little voice inside me would say I was wrong…I was so anxious about saying or doing the wrong thing I would freeze and do virtually nothing.

As this officer spoke to me there arose in me enough trust to listen. He told me to go home that evening and be with my wife and son. He gave me specific instructions on what I should do if certain things occurred in regard to orders for active duty, what my response should be and that I had to be determined and not become impatient. The thought of military police coming to my house to take me away did give me serious pause. I attended no more weekend meetings as a reservist.

Pickin Up the Pieces of Your Life

On September 17, 1971 I received orders to go on active duty or I would be considered AWOL (absent without leave) and be prosecuted under U.S. Military Code. On the very same day, as I was missing the last weekend drill my Honorable Discharge from the U.S. Army arrived by special delivery mail. I knew at that moment, that the officer that offered his assistance to me had kept his word. I believe all of this was a serious God Thing, though I wasn't close to serving Him at that time.

It was amazing. I had this sense of relief as I had been under a substantial amount of pressure and feelings of ineptness for several months. It was over. I contacted my commanding officer at the reserve center and told him about the discharge. I gave him my discharge number and returned to the reserve center a few days later to turn in my gear. I wish I could tell you I felt good about all of this, but I was disappointed I had not gone on to serve.

*****

After a couple of years where things were not so bad except for Eric's situation and the pressure that put on a young couple like us, we made a decision to make some drastic changes in our life as a family. What permitted this to occur was a settlement as a result of our accident. At that time the amount was considered substantial. It was more money than Mary and I had ever seen. It was designed to help us take care of Eric and it enabled us to do that. It also helped when I was between jobs during what turned out to be a very challenging economic and political time in our country. Initially we purchased a couple of new cars and a new house. Money was more readily available to purchase other items such as clothing, shoes, and other things we both needed and desired. But sadly it enabled me to purchase alcohol which only aggravated my addiction. I learned this lesson; it is way too easy to lean on money that is provided without the element of work. This is why I am so opposed to two years of unemployment compensation and virtually unlimited food stamps and other government giveaways.

In March of 1973 Mary, Eric and I moved to Albuquerque, New Mexico. Interestingly we took a map, I closed my eyes and I pointed my finger to the southwestern part of our country. My finger landed near Albuquerque, so that became our new destination. That was it, we took a preliminary trip to Albuquerque to find a house and a couple of months later we had a moving van move our furniture and away we went to the great southwest. It was our first time on U.S. Route 66 and across the Mississippi River…what an adventure. All of this took money which we would not have had except for the settlement. We were told by our doctor that the climate could help Eric and even extend his life because of the benefits of the sunshine and warmer weather.

As we settled into our new home in Albuquerque (it was very nice) we had to sell our house back in Ohio and made a few months of double payments. Finally the house in Ohio sold. I actually did well with employment, but my drinking became a much larger problem. What occurs unless stopped or mitigated in some way is a progression to drink more and more. When you are addicted you *may* not notice what is happening. You may wake up one day and ask, how did I get here, having to have alcohol or whatever the addiction may be. I can remember the progression and noticed the increase in addiction. However, I did not worry about it. That sounds odd doesn't it? But, when you are deceiving yourself and even having help to do so, you will just keep on indulging. Of course, toward the end of this time of addiction, I threw a counter punch by taking stimulants. When we moved to Albuquerque I was taking some valium that a doctor had prescribed to "settle my nerves." I was already in trouble, we were in trouble, but it just seemed the way life is or should be. This was not a big deal at the time nor a warning signal. I can tell you I have never been unfaithful to my wife. I have never been arrested or incarcerated, but I was an alcoholic and I needed help. It was only Divine intervention that protected me and kept me during this dangerous period of time. Drinking not only plays a part in destroying your life (it could kill you) but puts you in situations where you could do things that would destroy your family, and hurt others you don't even know.

Eric was doing OK in the warmer weather and we were able to put him in a school where Mary was a teacher's assistant. Facilities, care, instruction and equipment for the disabled were nothing then compared to today. I am not complaining, but those are the facts. Eric did have his tough times. We found out that he was a Strep (Streptococci) carrier and he had to fight some serious infections. I was in sales and on the road quite a lot. Most of my customers were hotels and restaurants which only gave me more access to alcohol. I knew chefs who were alcoholics, and they would make sure I had all I needed to drink at a very good price or for free. It seems that what I really didn't need was in abundance. I worked, came home, drank, went on the road and drank, I was really in trouble, and more trouble than I knew. My wife seemed to be patient and we seemed to get along OK. We loved our son and took good care of him, but there was more to life than this and I was about to get an education.

THINGS TO CONSIDER

Though I can trace my life and my activities, I still wonder how I was able to get in this mess with the alcohol. I believe firmly that my life is valuable. I believe it was given to me to do something special. I believe it is a God Thing! When I say special I don't mean being known by the masses and recognized by multitudes because of my place in the world. I am talking about honorable, important things with family, friends and vocation. I am talking about making the world a better place as a Christian with love, kindness and the ability to act on behalf of others who may be hurting in some way.

Have you been in embarrassing situations caused by your anxiety, fear and lack of confidence? Have you been embarrassed like I was? Torn between what you should and shouldn't do and what you did and didn't do? Think! What have you done about these things? How did you react? Could you have done better? How? If you haven't experienced this yet, after reading my story in this regard what would you do now if some situation came up? Think! Write a few notes.

_____

_____

_____

_____

_____

_____

_____

_____

_____

_____.

Pickin Up the Pieces of Your Life

Did you notice how I was blessed again? Are you being blessed right now and don't realize it? Think! If you are being blessed, are you showing your gratitude? Think! Write a few notes...

_____
_____
_____
_____
_____
_____
_____
_____
_____.

CHAPTER SIX

"THE WAY OUT"

It was the fall of 1974, Mary and I had been in New Mexico for about one and one-half years. One beautiful sunny day I was making sales/tech calls with a fellow salesman. He was a good example for me, someone to learn from.

We had just left one of our larger customers and as we turned to go on the highway I looked down and watched my hand shake. It was weird, I knew it had happened before, but that day I saw it for what it was, I needed a drink. As I recall it was not yet 11:00 a.m. and the truth was that though not every day, but most days, I had already had my first drink of alcohol, usually liquor. But this day I realized that something was not right and I wouldn't be able to get a drink until noon after we had made at least one more sales call. The truth is, I was anxious and worried about getting that drink. This was something different (or maybe I was just able to see it for what it was), regardless, it made me very uncomfortable. The truth was that I would always manage to get a drink when I wanted it, but today it didn't happen.

I managed to get to lunch and have a drink and all was OK, except the experience had shaken me. Just know that when an addict wants something, they want it now! A few minutes wait can put a person over the top when the "Toxic Crew" is working in your life.

It was October and I can tell you that the month of October was a miserable time for me. Something had changed and more was getting ready to change. I seemed to have an awareness of what was going on in my life, like never before. The shaking of my hands had my attention that day and I was on the road to being rearranged.

I don't recall the exact day, but by mid October I was home most every night because I wanted to stay home, pray and get right with God. By mid November I had necessarily left my job, because of the negative influences I encountered. I called upon restaurants and hotels and each of these places had bars where alcohol was plentiful. In addition, I had friends that I had business relationships with that were drinking as much or more than I. I knew instinctively that I needed to separate myself. This was a good job and I did well, however, I had come to the realization that I could not continue. The job was important, but not more important than my well being. I was catching on to what had happened in my life.

During this time, there were many nights after dinner I would take our son Eric and go in the front room and play Christian Music on the stereo. I would hold Eric, talk to God and cry. Mary was around, but busy doing other things. During these times Eric's shirt would be wet from my tears.

This is very important! I knew I needed a change in my life and sensed that it wasn't just an addiction to alcohol or tobacco or a few stimulants it was much deeper than that. I have told friends of mine who are in AA that the difference between them and me was they went to AA to get free of their addiction and in turn improve their life. I went to Jesus to improve my life and in turn my addictions were removed. I have never called myself a recovering alcoholic, because I was delivered from the addiction, I am not an alcoholic and I am not recovering.

Some have told me that experiences like I had are rare. I disagree, Jesus Christ did a remarkable work in my life, and it was obvious. I had seen and heard of this happening to others and it had now occurred in my life. He changed me so dramatically it was and still is unimaginable. In that regard people have told me that I wasn't addicted but simply abused alcohol and amphetamines. Let me tell you that being an alcoholic is not pretty. When you get behind a mask, a facade as I did, you are only fooling yourself. I can tell you of stories where I drove for over an hour and remember nothing about getting in the car, traveling, getting out of the car, walking into my house and getting into my own bed. I can tell you stories about being lost while out driving in the fog and having the fog part right at my street so I could get home. Believe me, blacking out, doing and saying stupid things that impacted others, having bodily functions out of control while in a drunken stupor were all a part of my life. Few if any knew about this, but these things happened over a nine year period of my life. I could have lost my family, I did lose money, could have been injured seriously and so many more bad things could have happened except for the Grace of God. I can only tell you I know Jesus and He is always awesome. Even with all of my faults and weaknesses I am so much better today than then, and it is immeasurable by human standards. Since my conversion I have met many people who have had their lives changed as dramatically as mine. These things I know, because they happened in my life... they are real.

I had two more experiences during that time that were both stupid and embarrassing and equally profound. The first was in November 1974; I had left my job because I no longer wanted to be tempted having alcohol so easily and readily available. One day I was driving home from a job interview, and I stopped at this bar. I walked in to get a drink and there was this film being projected on the back wall behind the bar; it was vulgar, just terrible. I went on in and ordered a drink and something inside me said, "If you stay here, you will never be the same." I didn't take a drink and I did not pay for the drink I had ordered, I just got out of there.

Now you should know that in the past months even before the "shaking hand moment" I would get drunk and I would stop by this small Pentecostal Church late at night and try to talk to the pastor, but I was just fooling myself as I would go out and drink again. But something was happening to me. It was a force that I couldn't deny, I would try, but I couldn't. I was finding out that the power of Jesus Christ is just that, POWER. I was changing, I continued to drink and smoke some, but much less than before. The truth is I could have quit at anytime, I had lost interest in alcohol, tobacco and amphetamines.

The second occurred near Christmas of 1974; I went out and purchased liquor for the Christmas Season. It was all discounted in price, but I still spent over $100.00. By New Year's Eve I had drunk some, and thrown the rest of it away, it was over. I cleaned the house of booze whether liquor, beer or wine. I packed up my pipes and cigars and gave them away, anything that was a part of that culture that I was indulging in and was not good for my health, spiritually, mental/emotionally or physically, I was done. Something big had occurred; Jesus had come into my life.

The greatest part of all of this was the realization that I had been forgiven and delivered from so many evil and simply unhealthy addictions, habits, thoughts, attitudes; and had been delivered into the Kingdom of God through Jesus Christ. This Kingdom is the opposite of the world I was living in…it was a good, a very good place to be. But, more was to come and it did, rapidly. All of sudden I was going to church whenever the doors were opened and even when they weren't, and doing so at the Pentecostal Church. In February of 1975 I was hired to sell welding alloys and began traveling more with some overnight stays. But my world had changed so much, that I would get something to eat for dinner and go back to my room to pray and read the Bible. On February 18, 1975 when I was in Gallup, New Mexico, I was praying to God and I had a Book of Acts experience. I was now in a very different world and there was no turning back.

Becoming a Christian does not mean we are perfect, I am not. Though changed, I still made mistakes and still do to this day. But I have a check in my spirit and if I make a mistake I confess my sins and repent (turn away) from what I did wrong. I then move ahead to be more pleasing in His Sight, (I Jn 1:9).

Jesus never leaves us, it is remarkable. Often, when people are converted they have done really nasty things. Now remember, I had my problems and they were serious, but had never been unfaithful to my wife, never been incarcerated, never lived on the street. But, my life was miserable in so many ways and I was very close to going into the abyss from which I believe I would not have returned. Things going bad usually take a while and the power of sin and its nasty ingredients get into lives and one day a person wakes up (hopefully) and says oops, enough is enough and I need help. I was able to do that!!

*****

Let me add another wonderful story to this already wonderful story. I am not sure how my living a life for Christ impacted my wife. She is very quiet and reserved unless she is talking about our family members and these days our grandchildren. But when I was converted, the change was dramatic. After a couple more years in New Mexico with things going well, we decided to move to Austin, Texas. In Austin there was a church that was large and full of life, and one in which I thought my ministry would grow and be further defined. The Church was one that had many members who had come out of the drug culture in Austin. There were a number of students that came to the church from the University of Texas. It was hard for Mary to leave Albuquerque, she and I both enjoyed it there. I was able to transfer my job to Austin and things again miraculously worked out. We were "cookin," so we moved to Texas.

We were only there a year, but during that year a lot of things occurred. It was a big time of testing for the Johnson's. Our son Eric began having seizures and this added to his already challenging mental and physical condition. We had a Golden Retriever that began to have seizures and ultimately had to be put down on Christmas Eve that year. We had an infestation of fleas…that is terrible when you are allergic to them and I was very allergic. But not long after we arrived in Austin a real miracle occurred.

It was a Sunday evening at Church, we were standing along with everyone else as the worship and praise to God was ringing out. There were about 1500 people there and one woman heard from God. She was sitting on the other side of the Church from us. To reach us she had to walk up one isle from the front to the back, across the rear of the Church and then from the back to the front down the aisle where we were. She walked in front of me and told my wife that God wanted her to go to the front of the church and be prayed for. She went up front and within seconds she had the same experience I had in that Holiday Inn in Gallup, New Mexico, it was a Book of Acts experience. We were now a different couple…we had been made new in Christ. What does that mean? We were changed. Our perspective on life had changed. We now wanted to and were serving the Lord Jesus Christ; and not merely stumbling through this world without regard for the one who created us.

I was a zealot when it came to my faith. I thought everyone should come to know Jesus. Immediately after I was converted I really felt I was supposed to minister as a preacher. That meant preaching wherever I could, whenever I could. I studied a lot and the church I was attending had a ministerial licensing program. I began to take advantage; studying the Bible, listening to my pastor and other preachers was exciting for me. I found it really hard to focus on other things with this fire burning within.

From 1973 right on through to 1979 we moved our residence several times, Ohio to the southwest United States; New Mexico and Texas and then ultimately back to Ohio. There were also moves from house to house while living in those places. This all occurred in 6 years.

After 1974 I was living a changed life in many ways. No drinking, no pills, I was kinder, more responsible, but just not seeing the success in finishing my education, and finding my dream job, whatever that meant. My sister Becky came to live with us in New Mexico in 1974. She loved our son Eric and was a great help taking care of him during that time. She attended an all girl's school, did well and loved New Mexico.

If you love and care at all for your family, especially when you have a sick child you can get emotionally drained very easily. I prayed a lot and believe I talked <u>at</u> God a lot but did not listen and rest in Him. At times fear was strongly impacting me. I can tell you today that faith is the opposite of fear and fear believed is faith contaminated. I believe Christians are often beat up by evil which uses out of control stress leading to anxiety, fear, doubt and depression as primary weapons. We need to learn as Christians that we can fight this battle and win! I finally did!

*****

From 1974 to 1979 I took advantage of some profitable employment opportunities. Nonetheless, though doing better in many ways I still felt that something more was planned for my life. I had this desire to complete my formal education and to get into that dream job. When Mary and I were both 29 in 1979 some things occurred that changed our lives and set us on a different course for life.

Over that five year period I was preaching whenever I could. I was able to preach in local churches in Texas, Florida, New Mexico, West Virginia and Ohio. We even started a small Church that met in houses. I had worked for a large corporation, I had worked in state government, worked for a small business lobby organization, and in between had worked selling energy efficient light bulbs, overhead doors, freezers and frozen foods and Indian jewelry. I had a Christian Radio Program that was on several stations and I even tried detailing cars. I was not lazy. I didn't hang around long in a job if it didn't produce an adequate income. My sales jobs were often commission sales… income was sometimes skinny.

Everyone has times in their lives (either sooner or later) where things just don't go well. Depending on how a person handles those times will often determine their future. Certainly having money saved to survive a bad financial situation will help. Having a good break manifest itself and being able to take advantage of it can also help. Sometimes just being able to survive, just to stand, endure as a family against whatever is standing in the way, will be the critical difference. Just know that if fear rules; you are going to be in trouble one way or the other.

I did some things right and worked hard but when confronted with something too new or challenging I would become stressed experience anxiousness, be fearful and quit. The addiction to alcohol and the nasty language were gone. My thoughts were cleaned up, anger and jealousy and vain ambition were not the problems they used to be. But neither Mary nor myself had this peace that we were looking for in regard to my career and where we should call home.

In the summer of 1977 after struggling financially and generally struggling to find more direction in our lives, Mary, Eric and I returned to Ohio to live. We had prayed about it and found peace. It just seemed right to return home to be close to family and find a new start. That's interesting isn't it? We left our home several years earlier to find a new start and then we returned back home to find a new start. Life can be very interesting and ours was just that.

SECOND PIECE OF MY LIFE PICKED UP
- FREEDOM -

The second piece of my life that was picked up was a life free from the bondage of a sinful life and an alcohol addiction. I think anyone who misuses or is addicted to certain chemicals, food, nicotine, buying, hoarding, or sex knows the great relief they had when they were released from this addiction. If you are one of these and have had trouble finding the solution to your problem, keep reading, you will find what I found.

Let me tell you again that being an alcoholic is not pretty. When you can get behind the façade or the mask that humans try to hide behind you only fool yourself. Let me reiterate there were times when I drove for over an hour and remember nothing about getting in the car or traveling. I barely remember getting out of the car and going to bed at my home. Remember my story about being lost while out driving in the fog and having the fog part right at my street so I could get home? Believe me, blacking out, doing and saying stupid things that impacted others, having bodily functions out of control while in a drunken stupor were all a part of my life at one time or another. I want to reaffirm to you, I didn't simply misuse alcohol, I was addicted.

Please read carefully, be aware and see if you have any of these signs that indicate you are addicted to anything. You see from the time I was fifteen and had that first night of drunkenness, something simply came over me. I could have probably stopped right then, but I liked the unrealistic thoughts, the pretend world I would enter when I was drunk. I believe being anxious and fearful about lots of things and especially going to school getting good grades etc. made drinking and escaping from reality a good thing for me in my life. As I said earlier, the 60's were tumultuous times for me.

James W. Johnson Ph.D.

I remember a month before I met Mary, me and two other guys left on a Friday afternoon and headed for Niagara Falls. It was very late October or early November. We took plenty of beer with us but not much money. We travelled and arrived in Buffalo N.Y. really late that night, went to a major university campus at Buffalo and made our way into the Student Union where it seemed everyone was stoned. The purple haze was present and we were drunk. We hung around for a while and went back to our car and slept in the cold all night. We didn't run the car because we didn't want to waste gasoline. The next day after a cold night, we stole pork and beans, peanut butter and bread from a store so we could eat; we ended up at Niagara Falls. We spent some time there, did some stupid things and began our trip back home. We stopped at Cleveland Hopkins International Airport and ran around drunk, sliding down the long walkways and generally making fools of ourselves. Somehow, we made it safely home in the dark of an early Sunday morning. We had sidestepped/escaped any injury or arrest. Drinking really makes you do dumb things. I just wanted to convey how stupid this addiction was and how it had taken custody of me to a great extent. I continued drinking another 5 years after that and I know I escaped the claws of evil and harm many times and only by the Grace of God.

October of 1974 I began pickin up the piece of my life that had been under the power and darkness of alcohol addiction. For approximately 4 months before this transformation began I had been taking amphetamines which were very simply mood altering stimulants that helped me get started each day. I knew a Sous-chef at a very nice restaurant in Albuquerque who would supply what I needed. I took one each morning rarely taking any at other times, because I was preoccupied with alcohol. No one knew about this until after I was freed from the addiction.

This piece of my life is freedom from this terrible addiction and a changed spirit which led to a changed soul and a healthier physical body. When you are freed in your total being from an old life and all things have become new, you often realize just how consumed you were with evil and the sadness that only evil can bring. I felt freedom for the first time since I was a small child. I felt as though my life was different I wanted to tell everyone, and I did.

The piece I had lost was freedom. I believe that is why freedom of spirit, soul and body are so important to me. It was so wonderful not being tempted when close to alcohol, or being consumed with the thoughts of having to buy alcohol, or keep enough in the house so I didn't have to run to the store all the time to buy more.

I lost freedom because of alcohol and it's dominion over my life, but God gave it back to me and I have been free ever since. I will tell you that other things have come after me in my mind will and emotions. The Lord Jesus has delivered every time I have called on Him about any temptation; whether being angry, selfish, lying, worrying, or fearful. Though all of those things which try to track us down throughout life still exist and come at us, He delivers. I have found even when challenged in some situation, if I will simply take a deep breath and pursue Jesus' Wisdom, Love and Help; I am met at my point of need with Grace and Mercy. That is Good News!

Being human means that sometimes we try to resolve issues and solve problems on our own. Yes, Jesus helped me pick up a piece of my life that was lost. That piece was freedom and it is so valuable and important to me. I still have no words to accurately describe it. He never changes (Heb 13:8) and is only one request away.

James W. Johnson Ph.D.

THINGS TO CONSIDER

It may seem overly simple to say, but being aware of who you are, who you are becoming and what is going on in your life is a really good plan. I had gone for nine years and had become numb to many things around me. Most often, whether an addiction such as alcohol is a part of your life or not you probably go on with life; working, being with family etc. and don't pay much attention to what is really going on, you just live. Trust me, good things and those not so good are going on in all of our lives right now...BEWARE!

Earlier I told you some things that were real in my life as a part of my addiction to alcohol. They were not good and though I saw them happening it was as though I was standing and watching from afar. This is strong language, but evil has a plan for your life, just as God has a plan for your life. Evil deceives me, you, and everyone as we permit it and never tells the truth. You can be fooled, I was and so were Adam and Eve (Gen 3). I worked every day, had some success and though I drank both at home and away, life went on. Regardless of the sense of normalcy in your life...BEWARE!

Changing a bad habit is a good thing, have you ever tried? It takes time and persistence doesn't it? Most people say it takes at least 21 days to change. My point is, good things take time to be manifest in your life and bad things do as well, often more than 21 days. When I first started drinking and smoking I didn't like it. I liked the feeling from both but had to adjust to the taste and smell. Are you overlooking things that are not good for you? Are trying to adjust to doing something that is not good for you and you know will cause you trouble, but you just keep on working at it until you have fooled yourself? Listening to the wrong voice, like Adam and Eve, like me? When was the last time this happened to you? Is it happening now? Is reading this book helping you become more aware? Think! Write a few notes.

_____
_____
_____
_____
_____
_____
_____
_____.

Just some final thoughts: God's Grace overcomes the plan of evil. You can have freedom from your bondage regardless of what it is? My wife and I found this wonderful gift of life in Christ Jesus! Are you stressed, Anxious, Fearful, Doubtful and lacking Hope? Depressed, a lot or a little? There is a delivering power that is so very powerful that I cannot describe it. It is the love of God through Jesus Christ. Have you experienced His delivering power? Do you need to? Do you want to? Check out (Rom 10:10-14). Think! Write a few notes.

_____
_____
_____
_____
_____
_____
_____
_____
_____.

CHAPTER SEVEN

"BACK HOME AGAIN"

We planned our long trip back from Texas to Ohio. We packed up our belongings in a rental truck with a hitch to pull our second car and away we went. It was a hot summer trip, but we were blessed as we drove accident and incident free. Returning to Ohio was clearly the right thing to do. My sister Becky was with us in Texas for a while and she drove back with Mary and Eric while I drove the truck. As we drove into Ohio we began to get a sense that we were home...we felt that all was going to be well.

We made our decision to return to Ohio after I had returned from several weeks of preaching in Florida and West Virginia. Mary and Eric were staying with her mom and dad in Ohio during that time. I drove to meet her there and after a day of discussion with input from her parents and my mom, we made the decision to return to Ohio. Before returning to Texas we took a trip to Columbus to find housing. We found a nice townhouse in north Columbus off of Cleveland Ave.

About a week later we drove into Columbus on a very warm summer night and began to move into our new place the following morning. A day or so after we had moved in we were driving out of our parking lot to do some shopping; we needed drapes and other miscellaneous things for our new residence. As we were driving out of the parking lot we were shocked to see friends of ours from Albuquerque. They had moved to Ohio to purchase a business and we found that we were all living in the same townhouse complex.

As we renewed our friendship, he offered me a sales job. It was August, 1977 and this was a blessing. He hired me into a sales position selling overhead garage doors and parts as well as glass for commercial storefronts and doors. We did OK but the pay was not great...I was on commission and though my friend was more than fair, by November we parted ways. He and his family were very kind to us. In addition, the income I had earned during that time was much needed and appreciated. I picked up a few sales jobs including working for a pie company delivering pies early in the morning and even reconditioned cars for a business that was near our residence. It was an interesting time and in its own way very exciting.

Late in 1977, needing a more stable income, I contacted a couple of old friends. One was a legislator and the other was working primarily with the governor for the State of Ohio. When I went to them for help, they didn't blink. They immediately put things into play and by January of 1978 I was working for the State of Ohio. I started out immediately in the Minority Business Development Office as a procurement officer. Shortly thereafter, I was asked to move into a position with the Ohio International Trade Division as their Public Information Officer.

In 1978 we were able to have money released that had been set aside from the cash settlement as a result of our accident. This made possible the purchase of our house in Reynoldsburg, a suburb of Columbus. Buying this modest house was another blessing. It was very nice and I do remember the interest rate on the loan as being 11.5%. Ouch!

With this job and a house of our own we were starting to gain ground economically. The pay was good, the benefits were equally as good and I liked the work. The house was more than adequate…things were going in the right direction. But something occurred that is hard to explain. As we headed toward the end of the year, I became anxious. I cannot tell you what it was, but I was anxious. Maybe the potential for success, maybe I was just supposed to leave, but, I began looking for other work and left. This is what was going on in my life. When I left this position, Mary was very disappointed.

In the summer of 1977 when we arrived back in Ohio through late 1979 I was actively engaged in ministry in addition to my regular employment. I pastored a small group of people. We did not meet in a formal church building, but we did meet in homes and occasionally a community center at an apartment complex. I baptized a number of people in a local river, a swimming pool and even in bathtubs. I was unsure where all of this would end up, but I believed strongly it was the right path to take at the time.

I also produced and hosted a radio program; The Jim Johnson Show. It was similar to the Larry Black Show that utilized air time on radio frequencies that ware available for public affairs programming; the program was on in my hometown of Upper Sandusky. I would do it live there and we would tape (reel to reel tape) it to send to other stations. Over a period of one year we went from one to eight radio stations all located in Ohio. These stations were connected by two closely associated business partners. It was a Christian Program playing contemporary Christian music of that day with a blend of selected secular recordings. It was a half hour program. I had listeners writing me from their homes, businesses and even from prisons. That went on successfully until I had the opportunity to extend to twelve and then to twenty stations, I froze, fear engulfed me and I just left it all behind. At the time I used a number of excuses but the truth is that the "Toxic Crew" had a way of just stepping in and I would fall for its threats and lies. My faith had been contaminated by fear.

*****

In very late 1978 after I had left my position at the State of Ohio I began working for a well known and highly respected small business lobby organization. I traveled an area well within a couple of hours of my home that included the Columbus - metro area and a more rural area east of Columbus. Each day I would arise, pray, go get in my car and start selling. I would visit our current members and then attempt to add as many new members as possible. I would put 30 Navy Beans in my left coat pocket and as I made calls each day I would not quit until I had passed all the beans from my left to right pocket. I did well. I called on all types of businesses. There were those with a hundred employees but most were mom and pop businesses. They were good people working hard for the American Dream.

One day I walked into a shoe repair shop in a small town just east of Columbus. The owner was a member of the organization I represented. The day I stopped by I saw a pair of two tone brown shoes in his window. They were high end real patent leather, and if they had been new, they would have been very expensive. I went in and tried them on. They were my size in length but the wrong width, too narrow. The person who owned them had left them there months ago. This business owner looked at me and said he would sell them to me for $10.00, $10.00? I couldn't believe it. I bought them and each time I wore them my feet would hurt, but they looked so nice!! I really believe this was a God Thing, but at the time, though thankful, I just saw them as a pair of shoes I could wear when I dressed up.

In the summer of 1978 I finished coursework in business management that I had started several years before. This was really important to me and Mary helped me finish as we struggled in the heat of Central Ohio. This was a real accomplishment for me. I completed all of this through correspondence (today it would be online distance learning) and received these two beautiful diplomas, I was excited. It was the first course of study I had finished since leaving high school ten years earlier. For the most part I had failed at all of my other educational endeavors. This was truly a milestone. I even received a school ring which I still have today.

In January of 1979 Mary gave birth to a baby boy; we named him Peter James Johnson. We had lost a child via miscarriage a year and a half before, but everything went really well with this pregnancy. Pete was born healthy and we were very happy. It was challenging to take care of two babies, but Mary did a great job... she was disciplined and loving, a really good mom and wife.

My income was sufficient and I seemed to be building a viable territory. Then the bottom fell out and I wasn't closing any sales, I was frustrated. I was praying for help and guidance. Going out each day and making thirty contacts a day is hard work. It can be fun when you are making sales, but I wasn't. We continued to struggle in this regard and I was getting frustrated.

As I write this I find myself shaking my head in frustration as I did during that challenging time. The summer of 1979 was five years of a New Life in Christ. My wife and I were both Christians and we could sense strongly the improvement in our lives. Our son Eric who was a sweet and gentle boy was now eight years old. He remained in diapers and we were maneuvering to keep him in the appropriate educational program. Our priority was keeping him safe and secure as well as giving him a lot of love. It is the rare family that has a sick child that does not sense at least some fear and doubt concerning the future. There is a remedy for this, though as a Christian I didn't really know and understand it at the time. Hint, the answer was to be found in the Word of God.

Going into the summer 1979 my work representing the small business lobby group was getting tougher and tougher. I sold memberships and had done alright earlier in the year, but in July we were really struggling. So Mary and I made a couple of decisions. The first was that I would go to a Fortune 500 Company located about thirty miles south of where we lived and apply for a sales position. One of my cousins had been employed there, and I was familiar with the business. I had also met a person who was a vice president of their international operations at a luncheon. As a courtesy he let me know that if he could ever help me, I should just contact him. I believe he was speaking in the context of business, but I took it personally.

*****

It was a very hot and steamy 95° day when I decided to put on a suit, tie and those brown patent leather shoes to go visit that company to obtain my dream job. I dressed up with my big four page resume which told about every job I had for the last nine years and had typed on my portable typewriter. The resume was just not fitting for presentation to a Fortune 500 Company. We were going to give it our best shot. I say we, because Mary and I prayed together over this opportunity and she helped me prepare for my presentation. We were tired and had no one to lean on but Jesus, so we did. Mary and I prayed one final prayer together. I kissed her and hugged our boys, got into a rather beat up green 1971 Chevrolet that had a manual transmission and no air conditioning (I left the better of our two cars for Mary to drive), and I was off to procure my dream job.

You should know that this was really an act of faith. No one would ever bet on me getting a job with this company knowing my work and education background. I was not a bad person and I could certainly do the work, but for the most part they hired college grads. I was twenty-nine and had more sales jobs than could be counted on two hands and I had graduated from a correspondence school.

As I drove there I was sweating, really sweating. I had taken my jacket off, but I was soaked. My beautiful shoes were so *tight* that when I pushed in on the clutch to shift it felt as though my foot was in a vice, it was painful. I arrived at the world headquarters of this company and walked into the main entrance. The receptionist guided me to the office of the man I needed to see. When I arrived, He was sitting right in front of me…I didn't have to get past a secretary to talk with him. The air conditioner in his office had stopped working so he was in the showroom where it was cool. Is this a God Thing or what? He seemed to remember me. This is where a connection I made when I was with the State of Ohio really worked to my advantage. We talked some and then he made a phone call to the person who oversaw the sales department. In a few minutes I was talking to a man who was going to change my life and neither he nor I had any idea what that was going to mean.

THINGS TO CONSIDER

I can only tell you that seeing our friends from New Mexico now in Ohio and him offering me a job was eye opening. We felt it was a God Thing! Then my friends coming together to find me work at the State of Ohio was a huge blessing. I think the move was meant to be and I give God all of the Glory for helping us. We had our challenges, but who doesn't? The key is that I was able to identify God's handiwork, in the midst of all that was going on.

Have you had a time that just seemed to be hectic and full of challenges yet you saw God's Hand in the middle of it? It was somehow working out? Think! Write a few notes.

_____
_____
_____
_____
_____
_____
_____
_____
_____
_____
_____
_____
_____.

So we now have two boys. We were a much happier family as things were going well on lots of fronts. You know we prayed a lot and trusted Jesus Christ for our needs to be met and to bring us peace. He did His part! We paid our tithes and gave offerings from our income. We were doing fine.

We took a big step of faith. Have you taken a big step of faith? Not knowing where the next dollar would come from but just knowing that somehow you were going to trust God to show up and show off? Think! Write a few notes.

_____
_____
_____
_____
_____
_____
_____
_____
_____
_____.

CHAPTER EIGHT

"THE SUMMER, THE WAIT AND THE VICTORY"

It was a hot summer in 1979, did I mention that? I was really hot, especially driving around in a car that was not air conditioned. We had one air conditioner for the entire house that was in one of our casement windows. It worked and worked to keep us cool but was really overpowered by the heat. We kept fans moving the air and both of our boys seemed to do OK. I was always hot and Mary seemed to just get along not saying a lot except for the occasional, "it's really hot." As the evening cooled down we eventually we fell asleep.

*****

My visit to the Fortune 500 Company was an act of faith. My resume was really poor in my opinion, it was a lot about nothing, but it was all that I could offer. My formal education was weak compared to others who would apply at that company. But, I was a salesman! I was applying for a sales position, which I did not know existed except by faith. My family needed me to perform. I remember my wife giving me a kiss before I left to visit that company and find work.

So there I was, walking over to visit a man named Larry. He was older, with some gray hair, handsome, had a deep voice and I would find out was a nice person. He and I had some things in common...he would change my life.

I was a bit embarrassed by my unsettled background and he acknowledged my resume was weak. It was interesting that Larry was in the U.S. Army during WWII and for a large part of the time he helped with big projects such as the Bob Hope visits to our troops. Bob Hope was a master entertainer who was committed to our country and our troops and he did untold wonderful things during very tough times for our troops and their families. What this did was give Larry and I a connection as I attended military school and had been honorably discharged from the military. He dressed nice when he was a soldier and he dressed nice now. There are certain disciplines once established you never forget nor ignore and dressing nice is something he never forgot. I also dressed nice (remember the shoes?) He inspected me as I was in my dark blue suit with the white piping around the pockets and lapels. I looked nice though my feet were killing me. We hit it off.

He told me there were no guarantees. He wasn't sure I would make the cut for a sales position, but regardless, he sent me around to visit with the marketing managers which took about an hour. After I left, those people in turn reported to him their thoughts concerning me. I found out later that without exception they all liked me and thought I could sell, but questioned whether I would be a good fit in their sales force.

When Larry and I parted ways that day he told me there were no openings; but there may be one in a month or so, that would mean late August or September. He told me not to get my hopes too high, and for me to stay in touch via phone every week. Our meeting ended and I left for home. When I got in the car, it was still very hot. I had left the windows down but the steering wheel was almost too hot to touch. Funny thing, I felt much better. I had seen something in Larry's eyes, heard something in his voice and had seen that smile that made me believe I should have hope, and I did.

When I arrived home after a hot thirty-forty minute drive, though guarded, I had encouraging words for Mary. To get that job would have been a dream come true for us. I would have a company car, a salary and a good bonus program. I was hopeful! But, we still had some issues on our plate. We had very little money which would not be enough to pay the house payment, buy food, pay utilities and some debt (though not much), and buy gasoline. I needed to talk to someone I trusted. I had an idea and it broke all of the rules that I had known in regard to making financial ends meet. No work, no money, no food, right? I had to visit my mom.

We put the kids in the car (the one with air conditioning) and drove about sixty miles north to visit her. Mary and I had discussed the subject of food-stamps; this was not like going out and getting them because somehow we deserved them as so many people do today. It was a really big deal. While visiting with my mom I broached this topic and was a little surprised. She said she wouldn't want me to take them if I didn't need them, but just as filler for a short time, would be OK. You see food stamps were welfare, they still are to me. Those of us, who work, pay the government money and they in turn hand it out according to their guidelines to "needy/deserving people." You can tell I still don't like this idea. I know there are people who absolutely need help and that is OK. I was still trying to figure a way around this big step. We talked a bit longer, ate dinner together and then drove back home.

The decision making process to take this big step was one of serious deliberation. There was a long held conviction in our families that food-stamps were welfare. Taking welfare was not acceptable. Secondly, there is an issue of personal pride in regard to the kind of person who takes food stamps. I thought my family and I were above that. Then there was the problem of what I would do until I did get a job? With food stamps do I still go out and look for work? Where? So we made a decision that we would get the food stamps for a short time and we would do what we needed to do to get me a job that would provide job satisfaction and of course provide financial security for our family.

The next day I went into Columbus to sign up for food stamps. I was not on unemployment compensation and had no income. Utilities and the house payment had to be made, and somehow we were able to work through that. Buying food was an issue unless we went to family and begged. I wasn't going to do that and thus we became the recipients of the food-stamp booklet. As I recall we had stamps for the remainder of July and I signed up for August as well. Eventually we had to sign up for September.

This was an embarrassing time for the two of us. We knew our children would not understand but our families did and I will tell you in many ways both of our families were cut from the same cloth. We were independent, hard working, money saving and compassionate people. We decided to close up our house. We paid the bills we could and as I recall, we had the phone disconnected. We were cutting our expenses, and needed to take whatever measures were necessary.

It was an important spiritual step for us as we stood by faith for this job. I didn't talk to other potential employers. We had faith that this was going to work out. I look back and know it must have been a God Thing because in the natural, I was probably not going to get that job. That is a faith lesson we all need to learn.

We stayed with mom. We painted her house, trimmed the windows and did some work inside and in the basement. It was an older house and could always use the extra care. We stayed with her and bought the food while she provided a place for us to stay and cut our expenses. It worked out well. She loved being with the grandkids and we enjoyed being with her and my sister. We also drove about 30 miles north and west visiting with Mary's mom and dad and then returned to my mom's house which was our new home base.

I phoned Larry every week and he always said, "Nothing new." We moved back into our house in late August early September and we were still living by faith. Then the day came, Larry called and said he would like to see me. He didn't have anything for sure, but wanted to talk to me. He requested I come down, I was nervous. This was it! I was going to learn about our destiny. I don't recall exactly how much we prayed over this but I am sure the Lord had an ear full.

I visited with Larry and still nothing for certain, but behind the scenes good things were happening. My record over these last few years wasn't as strong as either of us would have liked, but it was good enough. My references had responded favorably, though in all cases knew I had not reached my potential. I had potential and someone noticed? Yes! I left that meeting knowing I could not last much longer without a job and if I found a job it would not be like the one I was pursuing. Mary and I stepped out by faith and it looked like it was working.

I was told to call back on a certain day and when that day arrived I was anxious (excited, anticipating) and really wondering and hoping for the best. When Larry got on the phone he told me in so many words they had an opening and they were going to give me an opportunity to step up and reach my potential - YES - it worked...Thank You JESUS!!!

I was hired a couple of days later. I would have six months of training at the headquarters as and would be home every night, most importantly we would have a pay check! The first thing I tried to do was return about two weeks worth of food-stamps, that we I didn't need them anymore. Of course they had no process to intake issued food-stamps, so we bought food for another two weeks.

I started my dream job and it was wonderful to be working. We had made it. This was my dream job, did I already say that? I would have a company car, salary, and a good bonus plan. Our families were happy for us and my mom was proud of me; I was very happy as well. An interesting thing occurred when Larry told me that I had the position. He looked straight into my eyes and told me there were others more qualified than me. He also told me that he thought I had great potential and had great family responsibilities and that this may be my last real chance to succeed. He also told me with a quiet but firm voice that if I quit this job that he would personally see to it that I would never find another job in sales as long as I live, and he meant it. I did not let him down.

*****

The date is mid September and within two weeks I had my first pay-check. We were feeling better as some of the financial pressure was being released. October and November would be good months. I was maneuvering through the sales training maze at the home office. I would go from one department to the other and talk with the marketing managers, customer service people and of course spend a time in the manufacturing area. It was really enjoyable. I was learning a lot and people were nice. I often over-compensated, talked too much and tried to convince people I was capable of doing the job. All of that was unnecessary, but I thought it was. It was a bit stressful and thus I was a bit anxious. A few times fear raised its ugly head, but I kept praying and believing for good things and good things occurred. I should have learned from this in regard to the "Toxic Crew," but I wasn't there yet.

My family was doing fine. Mary was more relaxed even though you don't totally relax when you have a multiply impaired chil. We played with him and always looked for signs of improvement, though few and far between, there were some. Most important we loved to see him smile and sometimes laugh. It was by no stretch normal, but we had adjusted pretty well after eight years.

The holidays were fast approaching and for the first time in a couple of years we would be able to buy some nice Christmas gifts. Our baby boy Peter was doing fine and it was fun to see him on the floor with his brother. One was totally able and well and the other not so much, but they knew the other one was there. We were thankful for the interaction and enjoyment that brought.

*****

As usual, we went to visit our families during Thanksgiving. We went to my mom's house where she would invite one or two friends of the family. One was a cousin of my mom's who had lost her husband and another was just a friend that she and my sister knew. We always had a good time...great memories. We spent Thanksgiving Day at my mom's and then to Mary's family on Friday and Saturday, returning home on Sunday.

This year on the way back from being with Mary's family we stopped to pick something up at my mom's and to say hi. Mom was able to see the boys as we said good -bye until Christmas, about one month away. That was an interesting good-bye, because it would be Eric's last time to be with his grandparents and for them to see him.

That next week was tough. We had been audited by the IRS and each night I had to search through my records for receipts and documentation. Eric was on the floor with me as I worked. He would kick and move around. It was just nice to have him there; he had been there for eight and one-half years.

On Friday night November 30, 1979 before going to bed I gave Eric his phenol-barbital for his seizures as well as some decongestant. He had not been feeling well for a while. I can still feel the softness of his pajamas that he wore that evening. Mary and I prayed with him, kissed him and put him into bed.

In the morning of December 1, 1979 Mary had gotten up and we were planning on meeting with someone about diapers for Eric. He had been in diapers all of his life and we were now going to have to step up to larger diapers. She went to check on Eric and shortly thereafter she yelled "Jim!" Immediately I responded, "Is he gone?" Don't ask me why I said that, I don't know. He was gone. He had died through the night. I went in and briefly checked him and realized he was gone. A lot goes on in the moments after you find someone you love has died.

Pickin Up the Pieces of Your Life

You hold each other; you check on your other child, you ask each other what do we do? It is just a surreal time. We had to contact the police, someone. When we were able to get our bearings we decided to call the fire department which was less than a half - mile away.

I called and told them our son had died. I also told them they didn't have to turn their sirens on, because he had been dead for some time. The fireman was curt with me and said "do you want us to come or not?" I said of course, and he responded, "then we are coming our way." Quickly, I heard the sirens and it wasn't long before the fire department was there along with the Reynoldsburg Police, the Franklin County Sheriff, a City of Columbus Officer, ambulance and the medical examiners black van.

Officers talked to Mary and I separately and wanted the meds that Eric was taking. It was interesting that when the firemen arrived they came in the house running. We directed them to his room, but they didn't slow down at all. They had their bags and other things with them. As they went down the hallway to Eric's room you could hear those bags hitting the hallway walls. They made a lot of noise as they entered his room and then it became eerily quiet. One by one they walked out of his room, back down the hallway and by us. As they passed us they extended their sympathy. It was tough on all of us.

After everyone left and they had taken Eric's body to perform an autopsy, we began making those phone calls no one wants to make. I will only tell you that it was a long day and the next few days were difficult as well. Family members were crushed at Eric's passing. Neighbors were generous and caring. It was soon over...the funeral and all, and then it was time to go back to work and begin making the changes that are all so natural in situations like this. We were and are thankful for our faith in Jesus Christ; it made and has made all the difference to us during challenging times.

There are people that I encounter on a weekly basis that want nothing to do with Jesus Christ. They don't view knowing Him and being committed to His ways as being in a relationship with God. There was a time when I felt the same way. But, I learned firsthand and it was what sustained us through our challenging times, including Eric's death, that knowing Jesus Christ is not about belonging to a religion. When we were being threatened with overwhelming sorrow, grief and an extreme sense of loss, we found that it was all about knowing and understanding God intimately. We learned the true meaning of (Is 53:4a) as we felt Him carrying our grief and sorrow. I now know what is meant by "listening to what He has to say to me." I hear that voice deep inside me all the time. I have learned to listen and obey Him. He wants only the best for me (Jn 10:10).

*****

There were some adjustments that needed to be made in our lives. The son we had carried everywhere for eight and one half years was gone. No more carrying him to the car, lifting him into a special chair to be pushed somewhere. No more changing diapers. No more lots of things. We were adjusting to the first Christmas without him in eight and one –half years. The Christmas decorations that had his name were difficult to see and are today. Mary immediately packed almost all of his clothes to give away. She was now with Peter who was getting around everywhere and was really communicating more at 1 year old than Eric ever did. Life was different and we had great confidence that Eric was in a much better place; that helped us get through this difficult time.

Because of my new job we had more money to purchase Christmas gifts and that was great. The company I worked for had a retail store where employees were offered special discounts. Those discounts meant that our family members were going to get a lot of glass tableware, ovenware, beverage ware etc, and I think they all enjoyed receiving their gifts.

At work I continued in training and had been out in the field to a couple of sales offices. One was in Cleveland, Ohio and the other was Fort Wayne, Indiana where I met men that would be my counterparts when I finally went to the field. I was doing fine. I was hearing about the National Housewares Show that would be in January 1980 at McCormick Place in Chicago. I knew I was going to attend, but I had no idea what that was going to look like. I would soon find out.

James W. Johnson Ph.D.

"FROM FOOD STAMPS TO A CORPORATE JET"

There is a certain excitement and dread that surrounds attending a huge show like the National Housewares Show. Many marketing and sales personnel have to prepare to attend by making sure new product samples are ready to be displayed. Major customers are contacted, appointments for important meetings are set, and you get the idea. However, I had no idea what my part was going to be in all of this! The huge, very expensive display booth would be sent over on trucks and would be assembled by workers hired by the show officials. Our marketing people would then set up their displays of glassware products. So, what was I going to do and who would I work with?

About one week out from the event a couple of us who were in training were given our instructions. We would travel to Chicago, pick up rental cars at the airport and then be drivers for the company's executives. We would stay in a premier hotel in Chicago for several days making sure that the suite was taken care of with food and drinks for meetings. It would be the first time I was away from Mary and Peter and I really didn't want to go. This is where stress became anxiety, fear and doubt. I began to question if I should go or just quit. Why? Why would I leave a good job? I was able to battle the out of control stress, the Toxic Crew" lost and away to Chicago I flew.

Did I forget to mention, that my mode of transportation was not going to be a commercial aircraft? This is the interesting part. Five months earlier my family and I were on food stamps, just hoping, praying and believing for a good job and income. The day my wife drove me to the airport, it was a private airport and the aircraft was a corporate Jet. It was beautiful and I was going to ride on that jet to Chicago. Amazing!

Pickin Up the Pieces of Your Life

Because I didn't go out with certain people to drink and take part in other unseemly behavior, I did have some detractors. They remained my detractors for several years. But for the very most part I got along with everyone and I worked hard. While at the show I would be at our booth helping as I was needed. When executives were ready to go back to the hotel, I would be called upon, get the car, and bring it around to the appropriate doors. They would get in and away we would go into the Chicagoland traffic. It was busy, a bit nerve racking, but I enjoyed it. My guests never complained, so I began to feel comfortable with all of my duties, not just driving.

Early in the show I happened to be the driver for the CEO of the entire corporation, not just the division I worked for. It was a billion dollar corporation in 1980, which was big! I picked up the Chairman and his wife and away we went into the Chicagoland traffic. I was told not to talk to them unless they initiated the conversation. It wasn't long before they were asking me questions and we actually became friends.

When I reached the hotel there was a ramp that went to underground parking and was right in the front of the hotel. The ramp was also in front of huge windows where people would be waiting for valet service or just standing and watching people, whatever. As I approached the ramp I continued to move at a good pace and entered the ramp rather quickly. Guess who was standing in front of the windows as I came in, Larry. The gentleman who hired me and a couple of other executives watched as I "zoomed" (their words) past them with the CEO and his wife in the vehicle. As soon as I dropped them off, Larry was there to tell me I was driving too fast and I had better watch myself. But as the Lord would have it, the Chairman and his wife walked up to Larry and told him they wanted me to be their driver for the duration of the show. This was a good sign;

I was doing the right things. I was still warned to be careful and of course I would.

On one of our trips the Chairman asked me about my past and I spoke of my background in sales and mentioned that we had lived in Albuquerque, New Mexico. This interested him because they were looking for a location for a winter get away and they had considered New Mexico. I provided him with information about nice areas to live, where we had lived etc. Well the remainder of the time there was good. At the end of the week I flew home to my family on the corporate jet...still couldn't believe that was happening. Several times after that I flew back to Ohio with customers on that same jet and stayed in the company's beautiful guest house. I know there are those who didn't think twice about flying on that jet or being a guest in the guest house, but I was always amazed at where God had brought me from and where he had positioned me.

It was the spring of 1980. My first move was to Minneapolis-St Paul. Where we moved into a new condo. We had two cars that worked, a nice place to live and were in another stage of our new journey. We were having fun. I had to work hard, but I enjoyed it. It was the job I had always wanted.

Though we lived south of the Twin Cities, my first office was in Minneapolis. One day I was working back in our storage area going through some sample ware and I was told I had a phone call. Usually, they would take a message and I would call back later. As I walked toward my office, I asked the secretary who it was and she said it was the company's CEO. They were really surprised, I was pleasantly, but not unexpectedly surprised.

He was gracious and wanted to see how I was doing in Minnesota. He informed me that the mosquitoes there were as big as small birds, he was right. He also told me that it was much more hot and humid there than most people know, right again. He and his wife went to Albuquerque, searched for that winter home and though they decided on California, they joined one of the premier country clubs in Albuquerque. He thanked me, wished me well and that was the last time I spoke with him. I had great experiences and made a new friend in high places because he chose me as his driver at the National Housewares Show. The Scripture (Eph 2:17-21) comes to mind. What God was doing for me was out of His Abundance. He was going above and beyond what I could think or ask.

James W. Johnson Ph.D.

THINGS TO CONSIDER

Have you ever gone back over your life just to see how things really came together on your behalf? If I wouldn't have attended that meeting while I was working for the State of Ohio, I would have never met the man who would eventually help me get my dream job. I have wondered if that job at the State of Ohio wasn't for one reason, for me to meet that one man. Have you ever had something like that occur? Do you believe things like that can happen to you? I have had enough of these types of things happen to know for sure that God loves me even when I am not paying attention to the details of His Work in my life? Think! Write a few notes.

_____
_____
_____
_____
_____
_____
_____
_____
_____
_____.

How about me getting my dream job with less than great credentials? How about going from food stamps to a corporate jet? Being the chauffeur for the Chairman of the Board of Billion Dollar Corporation?

Because I have written this book I have reflected more on my life than I would have otherwise. Have you reflected on how

Pickin Up the Pieces of Your Life

you have been blessed? Maybe more importantly, have you given God an opportunity to bless you or have you gotten in the way of His helping hand? What does being blessed mean to you and me? Being blessed is experiencing God's favor, His kindness and goodness. It could be an unplanned pay raise or recovering unusually fast from surgery or any one of a thousand good things. Think! Write a few notes...

_____
_____
_____
_____
_____
_____
_____
_____
_____.

At times we had experienced loss in our lives. When Eric died we experienced a loss. It was as though we were on the verge of heartbreak, a trouncing. It was a mixed up time, but our faith in Jesus Christ gave us hope in the darkness. In your moments of darkness have you seen the hand of God working? Think! Write a few a notes

_____
_____
_____
_____
_____
_____
_____
_____
_____
_____.

I have found Christ to be "there" for me wherever "there" is. Mt 28:20... "I am with you alway, even unto the end of the world." (Acts 10:34b...)" I perceive that God is no respecter of persons..." What He will do for me or others He will do for you. (Heb 13:8) Jesus Christ never changes...That is Good News isn't it? He never changes, not one iota.

CHAPTER NINE

"A FAMILY THING"

For eight years I enjoyed my dream job. I had a wonderful office and showroom, lots of great clients and I won several sales awards; it was a good fit. In 1981 I was transferred to Grand Rapids, Michigan and we have lived in this area now for over thirty years. In 1986 I was let go from my position due to a corporate reorganization. They were fair to me in this departure process. In all of the years I was with them anxiety had been minimal. After losing my dream job, I must say anxiety did raise its ugly head, but just a little as I began to look for a new career.

It should be noted here that the "Toxic Crew" was not beating me up all the time while I was working my dream job. I firmly believe that when you are walking in the Will of God, doing what He wants you to do and where He wants you to be, you will walk in more peace than you can imagine.

*****

I had enjoyed working in sales and the financial security I had found. I had a good income, and earned a bonus each year which helped and the overall environment of work and the flexibility had made this a really wonderful employment experience.

In 1981 we had become captivated with the idea of riding bicycles a long distance to raise money for families that had a disabled family member. We created a Non - Profit Corporation called Tour of Hope Unlimited. For several years we rode an Annual 400 mile bike tour through three states to raise money for these families. We had other ideas as well and were able to implement them and give hope to families who had been like we were when Eric was alive. It was rewarding, very hard work and it was a family thing. Mary participated in the Annual Eric W. Johnson Memorial Bike Tour as a sag wagon driver and added much more to the effort with her hard work. Peter loved being on the tour, helping along the way and added this to his life story of interesting things he had done. It was a good time with challenges dispersed over the years, but we did help families with some of the things they needed but could not afford on their own.

In 1987 after losing my job, running the non-profit became very difficult. We were able to fund much of what we did in operations of the organization with a percentage of our income. When I was no longer working, this became problematic with the end being the shutting down of the non-profit. It was a sad time in many ways. I believe that economics played the primary role in my leaving this wonderful organization and the work we were doing. When I left others who had joined us in the work decided that if Mary and I were not a part of the organization it could not go on. We sadly dissolved the corporation.

It is hard to imagine what we could have accomplished if we had been able to continue. I can't blame anxiety and fear for this move. Again, there are just times when you must act, respond and the change that occurs is not always pleasant.

*****

It is always important to understand that change is going to occur whether you or I like it or not. In regard to the loss of my dream job, it is important to mention that some very special things occurred immediately following that event. First, the family that was closest to us as we developed and operated Tour of Hope Unlimited, emptied their freezer and brought its contents to our house. They wanted to make sure we had enough food. We had another friend that believed the Lord wanted him to give us $400 and he did. A local car dealer that had been sympathetic to our cause of helping those who were disabled and their families did something that really surprised us.

When my job was over and the dust settled, the company had of course taken the company car. That left us with one car. We needed another so I went to the dealership and talked to the owner. I told him what I was looking for and what we could afford. He told to look around on the lot.

Shortly thereafter he came to me in the showroom and explained to me he had found a car for us. He asked me if I had a color in mind and I said no. I certainly had a color I would prefer, but that day I was looking for a nice affordable car for our family.

He walked me over to a yellow Chevrolet Celebrity only a year old with low miles. It was creamy yellow in color. He then proceeded to offer me the car at a great price with affordable payments and nothing down. I called Mary and told her about it, she said OK let's buy it. I told him yes. He prepared the paperwork while I went to pickup Mary and Peter and return to the dealership to sign papers. As we finished signing the papers we looked for the date of our first payment, we were surprised. He had given us six months worth of payments. Our first payment was not until the middle of the seventh month from that day. What a Blessing, (I Tm 6:17).

Even though I had lost my dream job, God was working on our behalf and over the next year I took one job for about 6 months and was soon hired by a floor covering dealer to fill a newly created position. I stayed there for almost five years. By the way, a friend of mine helped network me into that job. I was better in regard to not letting stress get to me when this job came about. I should mention that while I was at the floor covering store, the owner loaned me the money to complete my bachelors' degree. In addition I was able, thanks to his flexibility to work part-time and earn my master's degree. After my academic failures the Lord worked it all out and I walked away from that place after five years having earned two degrees.

*****

I'm telling you about what occurred in my life after I lost my job, but something wonderful occurred in Mary's life as well. We went through a time of me settling back into a new job, as noted, it took a while. Again, I was looking for that better job and found it with the floor covering dealer. The owners were great and I owe them a lot. As strong Christians I look back and can see how they listened to God and helped me and my family.

In 1987 as I was just getting started in my job, Mary calls me over to our kitchen table where she was starting to fill out papers for school loans. She informed me she was returning to school to become a Special Education Teacher. She had taken a few classes in Ohio before we moved to New Mexico, but she hadn't talked about this much. She had been thinking about it. She started back to school in the fall of 1987.

In the meantime we sold our house and moved into a town house a couple of miles away. We were starting over, all of us. During this move we changed school districts so Peter was going to have a new school. It was exciting. I went back to school via correspondence in 1988 to finish my under graduate studies. That meant the entire family was in school! I admired Mary for her courage and determination and knew she would finish strong.

There are so many good things to say about my wife. She worked only short periods of time either full or part time between 1970 and 1990. She was a stay at home Mom. If you met our son Peter you would see the handiwork of a mom who poured into her son, it worked. She began teaching after graduating from college at age forty-one. She was thoughtful, and had always wanted to be a teacher, so she just did it. The time was right and she knew it. She had attended college after high school, but because we were married so young and then with life's ups and downs keeping priorities straight meant, no return to school. I admire her determination and she was very successful going on to earn a Master's Degree. She has now taught full time for almost twenty-five years. The Lord blessed us again, richly! I do believe that often being blessed by God takes some effort on our part. He may have a plan but we have to walk the path…take the journey!

James W. Johnson Ph.D.

NUMBER THREE PIECE OF MY LIFE PICKED UP
- EDUCATION -

As I write about my formal education and my attempts to earn an undergraduate degree, a brief update is in order. I have now earned an M.A. and most recently a Ph.D. I had the wonderful experience of graduating with distinction and my son graduated with high honors earning an Ed.D. We studied, travelled and attended classes together and graduated on the same day from the same school. I was sixty two and he was thirty-three.

As you know my academic efforts from high school until 1989 were poor. It is hard to explain how all of this materialized and my response to the challenges that always arose as I worked toward completing my formal education. I can tell you that a lack of confidence and the fear of failure were certainly issues.

I enrolled in seven schools before I was able to find myself working through the necessary final requirements to earn a post-secondary degree. All along the way I earned credits and they began to add up. I was a plodder.

In 1987 when Mary went back school, I decided to try again as well. Back then there were no online courses and webinars. Except for a few programs around the country such as "university without walls" and similarly named programs there just wasn't any real convenient way to earn a degree. If you didn't return to sit in classes, spend a lot of money and go through a long process you were not going to earn your degree. I was not prepared to be away from home while my wife was going back to school full time. It was my wife's turn and she deserved the support.

Do you remember when I searched for a military school and I found the name of the school in one of the popular magazines of the day?. In 1987 I did the same thing. I looked through some of the magazines and found an ad for a school that offered a Bachelor of Science degree via correspondence. This would mean studying on my own, sending in lessons and proctored exams. I had done that before and it had worked out, but it was all about me disciplining myself to finish. I gathered the information. I needed a specific number of hours earned plus I could get credit for specific, documented work experience. The balance of hours after the total already given credit for was what I needed to finish. The balance was nine courses and a major final paper.

I didn't have the money to pay for the coursework and I couldn't get a school loan so I spoke with my employer. He and his wife were great folks and paid for my education. As the payments came due, they took that amount out of my pay each paycheck until the amount was paid back. Over a period of two years I finished the course work and received my degree. It had been twenty years since I graduated from high school.

So, I had earned my B.S. Degree in Management with no intention of going any further. I was pleased that I worked hard and earned the degree. It was a positive thing for me personally and a piece of my life was picked up. It also got the monkey of failure off my back in regard to my education.

It was late in 1989 and I had a desire to go back to earn a Master's Degree. I checked around and found a program that interested me. It was a program in organizational communication at Western Michigan University. I visited the university in Kalamazoo, Michigan and spoke to the student advisor of the communications department Dr. Shirley Van Hoeven. I will never forget how kind she was to this almost forty year old person that had completed his undergraduate degree via correspondence school and had a poor academic record. I began to dream and then my wife and I talked about me returning to school.

Because this was graduate school (me going to graduate school - unheard of) I could actually arrange classes in the evening, no day classes required and the program was thirty-three hours. Mary just started teaching after three non-paying student teaching assignments and 3 years of course work. I would have to modify my work hours going to twenty-five hours per week. My employer helped again and if Mary would permit me to do this (we were sort of schooled out) I could earn a Master's Degree.

I offered this idea to Mary and told her what my income would be part-time. I had to get a school loan for about seven thousand dollars and I would have to do thirty three hours of course work. She laid out the guidelines and I would respectfully meet them. We needed to get on with our lives with improved income and hopefully moving into a house from our townhouse sooner rather than later.

She said OK, but you have one year to complete it - one year? I knew she was right so here was my plan. I applied for the school loan and received the seven thousand dollars needed. I went over the course work and my schedule for one year looked like this: one course early summer session, one course late summer session, four courses in the fall, three courses in the winter, two in the spring and I would graduate in June1991.

So the guy who had done so poorly was given an opportunity to go one step higher in his formal education. It worked, I was doing family things with my wife and son, working on completing eleven graduate courses in one year, working twenty five plus hours weekly and in the spring of the year needing and wanting to be with my Mom who had a serious surgery, I graduated. At one point I had a 3.7 GPA, at graduation I was at a 3.4 GPA. My dreams concerning education had come to pass. When I received my final transcript from WMU I read the transcript, where it stated that my undergraduate work had been poor.

I am thankful to God, my wife, employer and to Dr. Shirley Van Hoeven for giving me the opportunity and support to pick up this piece of my life.

I am convinced that when you begin to dream and plan to achieve a goal or pick up a piece of your life that putting it in writing is very important. You should write it down and look at it each day with a positive mind set and scriptural support. Since I have recognized the "Toxic Crew" in my life and especially when I see that there will be some stress in a situation, I always write down my plan, and believe I can reach my goal. I find it takes the pressure off of me. All I have to do is go back, read the plan I have set in place and follow it. I don't have to wonder and let worry and confusion enter the situation. Plan, write things down, follow the plan, it works. (Hab 2:2) in the Message Bible says "And then God answered; Write this, write what you see. Write it out in big block letters so that it can be read on the run." Even the scriptures demonstrate that writing down what is to be done and or what will happen is important. If it is good enough for God it is good enough for me, how about you?

THINGS TO CONSIDER

You will notice that anxiousness and fear were hanging around, but it was different this time. I had to earn an income and we had made some serious family decisions on moving forward. I had prayed and even cried over this situation. There was no room for anxiousness, fear, doubt, or depression to get us down, and that was the key. It was game time! Our faith was bigger than any fear. This is the way it is supposed to be!

Certainly there were moments of stress in all of this. But the stress was never released to cause that overwhelming anxiety, fear and doubt that had in the past so easily beset me. Have you ever had this experience? Have you ever used stress to make you stronger? Stress causes pressure and pressure on coal can make a diamond.

Economic times were not easy. Just like any time when there is a recession and or inflation or both, you don't have to make many mistakes before you find yourself in financial trouble. There is more than one challenge in all of this, but often I didn't do the right things. I should have asked God for wisdom, because He gives it if we ask. It seemed when things would start to go well I would get in the way. Better explained, I would find a "reason" to leave. There is a Great Lesson in this.

Today, we hear how tough things are…I can't pay my bills, I am out of work, I can't find a job, it isn't fair etc. etc. I have learned that the best way to stay out of financial trouble is to be vigilant. Keep your eye on the ball. Don't get into to debt. You don't have to have everything everyone else does. Really! It is true. Things go south, that is just the way life is sometimes. If you are prepared and if you have a strong faith in God and pay attention to Him, pray and stay in His Word, you will find things work out for the best.

One of the advantages of living in a nation that was built on Judeo-Christian Principles is that we have God and freedom to go to and learn about and apply His principles to our lives. It is like this big secret. But, it is no secret at all, one of the advantages of serving God and for me and my family serving Jesus Christ is that if we will pay attention, understand how He works and follow His teachings...not only our family but that of others will be much better. This is real success. For many of us we may be committed to a strong faith in God. We try to be pleasing in His sight, be good and honest and respect others and be wise in our every day dealings. But, I wonder how many of us really realize the POWER of God and the profound difference He can make if we really commit our lives to Him and acknowledge Him in all of our ways? Though I don't want to be judgmental, I think for the most part even Christians limit God. They don't get to experience what He can do in our personal lives, and in the life of our nation. We need to take time to learn more and then take action in this regard.

I recently tweeted: @Drjimwjohnson: "Jesus wants your attention; it gives Him something to work with! Pro 4:20-22 now that is Good News!" Have you given Jesus anything to work with lately? Have you payed attention? It is amazing the things that can happen if we will just pay attention to Him, listen. He has an amazing vocabulary of love, freedom, salvation, healing, prosperity and opportunity. Have you payed attention? Think! Write a few notes.

_____

_____

_____

_____

_____

_____

James W. Johnson Ph.D.

CHAPTER TEN
"A UNIQUE OPPORTUNITY"

This chapter brings us to a new and interesting time. After earning my M.A. degree and finishing several really good years with the floor covering company whose owners were a blessing to our family, a new opportunity had arrived. I hope you will think about this chapter and consider where you are and what you are thinking when something different and risky is offered to you. What will you do?

I had been involved for several years with the Republican Party at the local level. I had been a volunteer and a delegate to the state and county conventions during some interesting times in the late 80's. A good friend of mine, Glenn, who had invited me to the Michigan Republican State Committee as a proxy was now pushing me to pursue a paid position as a Republican Consultant. It would be in the 9th Congressional District during the election cycle of 1992.

This would mean that I would by faith take a temporary position (for one year approximately) and do work I had never done, but liked the idea of doing. It was late in 1991 and I had met with the local Republican leaders from around the congressional district and they decided that I was the person they wanted for this position. A portion of my pay would come from the current congressman and the remainder from other political sources, including state reps and senators who were in the congressional district.

Mary was willing to give this a try…so we did it. I held this position for about 6 months when the candidate that was seeking to unseat the current congressman offered me a position on his campaign. It was going to be a very low budget campaign. I was in tune with the political climate and understood he could win, though nothing was for sure.

Mary, Peter and I prayed over this opportunity for a day and a half. I had experience in advertising especially radio and print media. In addition, I had experience planning for and riding long distance bike tours. It just so happened that this candidate wanted to ride through the congressional district on a bike. It was a marketing strategy to show he was out with the people, the potential voters. He would meet a lot of people if we organized it right; and he would get plenty of free print, radio and TV time as well. After the day and a half, I said yes to the opportunity. Interestingly, he offered me the job for one month, with practically no pay. Thirty days was the time frame we had to win this campaign. He had some good help prior to my arrival and had established a good base for this campaign, but one month? If he won the primary I would stay on through the general election and possibly be hired as a congressional aide.

Well, we won! I stayed on through the general campaign and we won again. I was hired as a staffer and became his District Director. I would hire and work with others to open our offices throughout the district and then oversee a staff that took care of constituency requests and other related activities. In addition, an important part of my duties was to manage the congressman's schedule while in the district. I was also his campaign director for the next two campaign cycles.

This was an interesting opportunity. I met many interesting people such as the Speaker of the House of Representatives, other members of Congress, the President and presidential candidates as well. I have never regretted this move. It was one that was taken by faith. My wife and son were engaged with me a lot during those years, traveling and helping with events, I think we would all say it was a good experience.

Though a good experience, it wore me out. Politics are not all fun all the time. The hours were long and sometimes it seemed that the work was never ending. I was amazed how serious everyone took things political. Some were convinced that politics even at the local level were so important that it was worth lying and cheating for…I did not and that caused some friction for me with those I worked with who were affiliated with the Republican Party. This did cause some stress and there were times when I became anxious and even fearful. I did seem to work through all of it and again, over all, a good experience and one where my faith and that of my family's was stretched. I stayed on board until 1997 and then moved onto the nonprofit sector going to work for The Salvation Army until 2005

*****

The Salvation Army offered me the opportunity to minister and to be a part of people's lives in an important way. We had an unusual situation as we responded to the 911 tragedy on a local level at the Gerald R. Ford International Airport. We were able to get to the airport within about two and one-half hours

James W. Johnson Ph.D.

with water and food for those who were stranded. We stayed from Tuesday September the 11th until the following Saturday evening. I was the Information Officer in the Emergency Services Incident Chain of Command and was the lead onsite person for that project. This type of project was always a real team effort and I enjoyed being a part of the team. We had local businesses sending food. There were those who came and were willing to take people to their homes instead of them having to stay at the airport or going to a hotel. It was a moving experience I will never forget.

The most involved and totally rewarding experience I had was when I was given the responsibility of heading up Operation Home-Front Families when the Iraqi War began. I led volunteers to help the troops and family members of troops being deployed by providing useful resources. It was a great experience and I still have many friends and relationships from that very special time. I was actually able to continue helping by bringing another organization to help these families after I left The Salvation Army.

FOURTH PIECE OF MY LIFE PICKED UP
- ATHLETICS -

During the time I was finishing up my work with the congressman and beginning my time with The Salvation Army I was given the opportunity to coach high school track and field. Most important and most rewarding to me was the opportunity I had to coach my son. Coach Dave Bolhuis at Hudsonville High School gave me the opportunity to coach and he put up with me while I adjusted to being a coach. I worked hard, studied hard, and did my best to give all of our athletes the best high school experience possible. I coached two all state throwers one male and one female. While Pete was in college we coached together and he was a part of coaching a female athlete who was an all state thrower and went to the Midwest Meet of Champions.

I will be forever grateful to the parents, the school, the athletes and Coach Bolhuis for hanging in there with me and giving me this wonderful opportunity. During this time I became personal friends with Olympian discus and shot put throwers. This was a great time in my life. I was also privileged to help set up the workout/lifting program for The Salvation Army at one of their local community centers. For two years, as a part of a community education program I created and led summer speed and conditioning programs. My son carried out a strength program simultaneously. We compared notes, worked together; which was fun and very fulfilling. In addition, I was able to use some of my athletic training knowledge and skills.

As a result of working with high school athletes, I became acquainted with a high school football player who was looking at colleges where he could both attend and play football. He asked for my advice; I contacted Ohio State and explained to them I had been on the training staff back in 1969 and had an athlete for them to consider. They honored us including the athlete's Dad by giving us passes to the OSU Spring Football Game which was a recruiting event. This young athlete was able to meet the coaches and talk with them about going to Ohio State to play football.

When I left The Ohio State University in 1969 I was very disappointed and could not have imagined that piece of my life ever being picked up. This piece of my life was so enjoyable and fulfilling it is hard to explain. I do believe it was a God thing. Who else could put the pieces together so magnificently? This piece was different than the first which fell, (My Ohio State experience) and I am not sure how the original could have been any better than this.

FIFTH PIECE OF MY LIFE PICKED UP
- MILITARY SERVICE -

This piece of my life seemed almost impossible to pick up. How do you go into military service after years and years have passed? I mentioned before that life changes and the pieces of your life that may fall may look different when they are picked up.

I grew up meeting WWI vets when I was a small boy. Many had been seriously injured with mustard gas. WWII Vets of which my dad was one were abundant in my home town. My dad and I would go to the American Legion or VFW; see the vets and listen to the stories they told about being in war.

I grew up in the Vietnam Era. We lost several young men in Vietnam from our town and outlying areas in the county. When it came time for me to sign up with the selective service many young guys like me had to make the decision whether to go to college and get a deferment or go in the service. I had a knee injury and it was questionable whether I would pass the physical for entry into the military; with the OSU opportunity I decided to try college.

Long story short, I didn't qualify physically for the Air Force or the Navy my first choices, but did qualify for the Army. When the opportunity came to enlist in the U.S. Army Reserve, I took it. As you remember because of the automobile accident and the injuries to my wife my going on active duty was delayed. I received an Honorable Discharge but never did go on active duty. Though releasing enormous family pressures, I was disappointed I did not serve as I had hoped.

Over thirty years later I was chosen to be the Coordinator of Operation Home Front Families for The Salvation Army for the Western Michigan Northern Indiana Division. I wanted to do the job and be a blessing to our military families, but I had no idea how much work it would take nor did I realize how fulfilling the experience would be.

When our troops went into Iraq in 2003 I was called by Alpha Co. Marine Reserves to bring snacks and drinks for the families who were coming in for some encouragement and instruction on what to expect as their family members went off to war. That was just the beginning; I worked hard for the next two years setting up events for the families whose members had been deployed. I also worked to help a group of family members who started Operation Pillow Talk. People would sign and send messages of encouragement to our troops on pillows; and the pillows would then be sent to our troops. We also sponsored pre-deployment events for the troops, their family and friends. We made sure that those being deployed had reading material and food for their long trips on buses as they left Grand Rapids to fly to their first stateside location before going to Iraq or Afghanistan.

I left The Salvation Army in 2005. I did however continue to work with the families and especially Alpha Co. Marines. I stayed with it and was a blessing to the Marines (not as much as they were to me). I was used on one occasion to raise ten thousand dollars for a hospital in Fallujah, Iraq. Our Marines were helping the locals who were ill and injured and by virtue of that, our Marines were provided important real time intelligence.

Alpha Co. lost five Marines during that deployment in 2006-07. I was a part of a group of former U.S. Marines and other volunteers who constructed The Fallen Marine Memorial, which stands today in Grand Rapids, Michigan. I was honored a couple of times with certificates and once with a flag that flew over Fallujah. I appreciated the recognition, but these men payed the supreme sacrifice.

During this same time I was blessed to be a part of The WWI Survivor Project that a friend of mine initiated. He wanted to photograph and chronicle the lives of the last surviving WWI Veterans. There were nine remaining when we started the project. After much hard work with David DeJonge (who did the important work) my wife and I were invited to a ceremony at the Pentagon where those portraits were put on display and remain today.

The day of this event the last living WWI Vet that served overseas Frank Buckles was present. It was a room that seated about 500 people. Mary and I were privileged to have reserved seats. We sat in the second row behind the then Chairman of the Joint Chiefs of Staff Michael Mullen. Robert Gates the Secretary Defense presided over the event along with the Secretary of the Army.

Here is the point and it is clear to me. We are not to look back in our lives and live in regret about the past. It makes no sense. But there are times when pieces of our lives have fallen and we can see some of them picked up and though different in form, may be very rewarding and fulfilling like this piece was for me.

Though I was never on active duty, I now feel fulfilled in regard to service to my country and to our military personnel and their families.

THINGS TO CONSIDER

The opportunities that going into politics and eventually public service gave me have been rewarding. It was amazing how so many things I had learned earlier in life reconnected. It was an act of faith to make this step; and with my wife joining me in faith as she started her new career it was a very special time. When I started working on the congressional campaign I found that my knowledge of planning and participating in four-hundred mile bike tours through three states would contribute directly to his campaign. How did I get there at that precise time with the knowledge and experience needed for a thirty day congressional campaign? It had to be Jesus…it was a God Thing! In addition, who would have thought that my going to work for the Salvation Army would lead to a piece of my life being picked up.

Are you in the midst of change? Wondering if you should go about your work in faith? Or are you wondering if where you are is a dead end? Do you think maybe what you are doing now will be something you can use in the future, some other place and time? You could be surprised, right? Think! Write a few notes.

_____
_____
_____
_____
_____
_____
_____
_____
_____.

Pickin Up the Pieces of Your Life

I would argue that we serve an Awesome God. I believe that there are times when He has this plan and it looks strange to us and others around us. You may ask the question, what are you doing Lord? God says you are doing what He wants you to, what do you think about that? Think! Write a few notes.

_____
_____
_____
_____
_____
_____
_____
_____.

IDEAS ON PICKIN UP A PIECE OF YOUR LIFE

When you start, don't look back at your life with sorrow and grief regretting what was lost. My point in all of this is to move forward and to live a more fulfilled life. Pickin up a piece of your life is supposed to be a good thing. Make sure you approach whatever piece you want to pick up with love and faith. Have confidence that what you are going after will succeed, (Lk 11:9, 10).

Next, think before you act. For example, let's say the piece of your life that you let fall was learning to play the piano. You can do this right? You start working on how you can find a piano to use. Maybe you can find one at a good price or you have one but it needs to be tuned. Now be prayerful and ask for His help. He may make a piano available at your church that you could use to practice on or you may find someone who can tune your piano for an affordable price. Nothing is impossible. Find someone you could work with to give you piano lessons. If you can't afford the lessons, ask the Lord for provision so you can have the money to take lessons. Here is what occurs. When you are focused on this and invite the Lord Jesus in to help, He will meet all of your needs (Phil 4:9). Confess and believe that Scripture and look for good things to occur. Don't doubt, have faith. Without it you don't please God and you won't get what you want or need (Heb 11:6). When I found my dream job it was all about faith and positive action based on that faith that produced great results. It was the Lord and I working together... quite a partnership.

Make sure you don't let others who may not have your vision and desire discourage you. Learning to play the piano, go back to school, find and restore a 57 Chevy, or whatever it may be, is OK. Have that underlying confidence that it will work out.

Write down what you desire and look at that goal every day. Believe you will get it, don't doubt. Speak what you want out loud and use Scripture that applies to what you are doing. One day you will be playing the piano. Remember, the Lord gives all things to enjoy (I Tm 6:17), ENJOY!

PART II

CHAPTER ELEVEN

"PANIC"

We never stop learning! Never! The question for me is, am I learning the right things that help me become a better or healthier person? Learning is what we do that increases our knowledge or skill in a given area of life.

I began to learn new lessons back in late 2007, when I was 57 years old. The new lessons were about out of control stress, followed by the "Toxic Crew" of: anxiety, fear, doubt, and depression. How can that be? Applying these terms to me? Implying that I may have a problem with this "Toxic Crew" in my life? When you recognize them, when they show up, you have to believe they may have been hanging around in different forms and at times unnoticeable. They will get your attention just as they did mine; just don't get caught off guard.

As I write this section of the book I go back to just how much attention I was paying to certain things in my life. I am always on guard to keep my thoughts as pure as possible, keep my thoughts in order so I am pleasing to God and respectful of others. If you are a Christian you are probably like me and do your best to make sure your speech and actions are pleasing to God as well; most of us do those types of things. But when it came to the "Toxic Crew" I was not paying attention as I should. Even though I worked at being a good person and pleasing to God, there were times when I saw a cracks, even a deep crevice or two in my armor; this is similar to finding a crack in the fuselage of a 747 Aircraft. When that occurs a person better be paying attention and take appropriate action. You and I are to be doing the preventative maintenance of our mind, will, emotions and our bodies. We have to have to be on the lookout for dangerous warning signs. Lack of good observation and appropriate action may result in a crash or near crash…not good.

I am a nice guy. I can also be demonstrative when I communicate with others; however, my temper is balanced. Historically though, if I am pushed on an issue, something that has been done to me over and over again, I may display some anger. I am not talking about inappropriate language. The voice is raised, I become uncharacteristically animated, noticeably disturbed and frustration leaps out of me. During those times those who are receiving my wrath are often only aware of that event. Few see the many times I tried to resolve an issue. They see only the climax of weeks or months of frustration. These types of events have been rare in my life since my commitment to Christ. This is the Toxic Crew at work and after an event like this I feel so terrible, apologize and try to explain why I said or did what I did.

We need to pay attention: notice, contemplate, meditate, and think about, what is going on in our lives. I was not paying attention to the precursors of a panic attack. We need to pay attention. Any outburst from me was preceded by many efforts to resolve a situation that was causing me angst. But if we pay attention daily and look deeper, give thought to what is going on in our lives, we may not be nearly so surprised by a panic attack as I was in 2008. For that matter there may not have been any panic attack at all. I tell you today that I am much more observant in my personal life. By virtue of the real life experiences I have had with the invasive "Toxic Crew" I want to warn others, BEWARE!

The scriptures hold valuable nuggets of truth such as "Be sober, be vigilant; because your adversary the devil, as a roaring lion walketh about seeking whom he may devour;" (I Pt 5:8a). This is what I mean in part by thinking and being observant. Sometimes our thoughts need to be replaced by faith (Mt 6:25). If we will stay in the Word of God, listen to it, read it, speak it, and make sure it is deep within us and simply think, meditate, and be contemplative on the Word and its promises, Jesus will lead us into His truth. That means He will show us what we need to see, make us aware of danger and show us how to avoid the traps that are set by the thief who steals, kills and destroys (Jn 10:10). This was a huge part of my walk out of the darkness I was in. It simply took me time to really believe this was true. It wasn't God who was slow, it was me.

*****

Back to my situation in 2007 and early 2008, I was having trouble breathing and found myself anxious. I was coughing but had no congestion in my chest. The evenings became times where I was anxious, worried and felt as though the walls were closing in on me; I sensed darkness. This was a different experience for me; being anxious and having this darkness was not enjoyable. I was looking for a solution from God. But when you are anxious and worried your faith is being overcome by fear and doubt. Jesus said in (Mt 6) take no thought, take no thought... He meant, don't worry. He knew then and knows now that when we worry it means that faith and confidence in Him is waning. This is the opposite of the faith and confidence in Him that we have to have to live for Him. Without faith, we know that it is impossible to please God (Heb 11:6). When we let our faith become overcome by fear the "Toxic Crew" moves in for a knockout punch. We go to those in the medical and health care professions for help. They are willing to help as much as they can and they will probably begin helping by recommending coping strategies. If that doesn't work, they will probably recommend medication. It becomes very confusing especially if you want to trust God for healing and peace. When should medication be considered and taken? Is this a contradiction of our faith if we do take meds? These are legitimate questions to ask and in the meantime you may be in a battle that you may believe you are losing.

*****

As I reflect on my life since my conversion, I can see things today that I hadn't seen in over thirty years. This is really important; why didn't I catch on to the symptoms and why couldn't I see my responses were wrong if I was to have peace? Was I just fooling myself? Was I really seeing things and ignoring them? Was I scared of what I saw and overwhelmed by fear? Was my pride in the way?

I must say that pride played a part for sure and more than I would like to admit. What is wrong with having issues and working through them with God's help? Nothing! Then why don't we do that? Basically what I did was not understand what was wrong and how God could guide me through the challenge. Maybe the biggest mistake we make is running to professionals first and then God second. That doesn't mean that God doesn't have others in His family such as doctors and therapists that He may use to help us. The key for me was that as promised, He was there waiting for me; and when I went to Him for help he delivered. It is not easy to go to God first especially when the priority of those around us is to go to a physician first.

Some lessons are easier learned than others. In 2007 when I encountered anxiety and didn't even understand what was going on, I went to the Lord first and then to the doctor. I had blood tests, an EKG, and respiratory tests and nothing definitive was found to be wrong. I could sense the Lord leading me and I did my best to follow.

*****

In the spring of 2008 Mary and I were coming back from a weeklong trip in Ohio where we visited family and just spent some time in the Columbus, Ohio area. We visited the cemetery where our son Eric was buried. That visit is always emotional, but we did other things to enjoy ourselves as well. We did some shopping, eating out and a lot of walking around and relaxing. I thought I was relaxing, upon reflection and on second thought, probably not.

The day we returned from Ohio began with me finding a coupon for a free cup of coffee at this particular coffee shop each day for twenty days. This coffee shop is well known with many locations. I had a cup of coffee early as we began the day. As we travelled, I stopped at another one of their shops and had another cup and I repeated that a total of four times that day…I was soon to find out that the consumption of several big cups of caffeinated coffee was too much for me. Along with the other problems I had been dealing with for about seven months it was only a matter of time until the dam burst.

We returned home and as the evening passed I began to feel light headed; I was sweating, had numbness in my legs and arms and my thoughts were racing more than usual. The racing thoughts were a key – past, present and future – the problem was I didn't comprehend what was taking place. At 11:00PM I took two over the counter pain and stress relieving capsules to relax and went to bed. I woke up around 12:30AM somewhat disoriented and very nervous. My mind was racing like a supercharged engine, my chest was heaving and hurting, and I felt like my throat was closing. I had numbness is my arms and legs. I asked Mary to get up with me and told her I thought I needed to go to the emergency room. She took a few moments to gather herself, change clothes and before she did that, I had contacted 911 and help was on the way. Emergency vehicles with red and blue lights, a fire truck, the sheriff, and then the paramedics arrived; what a mess I had caused. Neighbors were awakened and I was the instigator. After going to the emergency room, having a CT Scan, EKG, EEG, and being monitored for a couple of hours, I returned home with instructions to see my doctor.

*****

A year later in late May of 2009 I had a series of panic attacks over a two day period. I had Mary take me to the hospital – same routine as before – this time they suggested I may have had a seizure – again, go see my doctor.

Before I visited my doctor, a pastor friend of mine had me take an ADD self-reporting exam. It revealed the very symptoms I was having and had for years. When I went to the doctor he explained that ADD and anxiety had some similar characteristics. I found this to be interesting. How do you know which is which. He gave me a prescription and if I took this particular drug I would know quickly if I was dealing with anxiety or ADD, but after praying some more I decided not to take the prescription. I am sure this would have been OK, but I was doing my best to lean on God. Throughout my Christian Life I had found that Scripture holds the answers...I stayed in the Word with great focus.

On July 4, 2009 Mary and I were at a local parade and as we watched, a large motor home came by with a banner on the side that read, "Reclaim Your Brain." There were people walking along side handing out brochures. They came right up to me but handed the brochure to someone else and moved on. That meant I would go home and look up "Reclaim Your Brain" online. After finding the "Reclaim Your Brain" website, I found that they were going to have an information meeting at a local seminary. I attended the meeting and learned about neuro feedback which focused on brain, heart and respiration function and explained many of the issues I had been experiencing since a child.

My family physician and I discussed my symptoms, and suggested that I start with tests to eliminate the potential of other serious problems. The first would be a stress test to check my heart. After the stress test, I received a phone call from the cardiologist. They had found a problem and wanted to do a heart catheterization. The thought of that made me anxious, but the results showed a false positive and I was just fine. Later in the year I had a colonoscopy and a prostate biopsy; both tests were negative. During that time I began neuro feedback sessions, and my improvement was noticeable; this was an answer to prayer. I began to learn more about the brain and how as a human I am fearfully and wonderfully made (Ps 139:14).

As I learned more and more about the brain, what it could do and why it did what it did and how it did it, I also understood why Jesus told us not to worry; my level of anxiety had changed dramatically. If a high stress situation should arise, I see the negative and toxic thoughts begin to materialize from afar off. That is my heads up! The Lord has taught me how to adjust. I adjust so naturally now that the stress and potential attack of the Toxic Crew don't even get close. I don't take any medication and that is really good news!

This is hard to explain to others who continue to struggle with overwhelming anxiety, fear, worry and depression. Now, I pay attention; I know I win with Christ. It is spiritual warfare to me. I know it sounds simple, it's not, but it is. Jesus remains the answer for the troubled soul (Jn 14:1).

THINGS TO CONSIDER

Are you paying attention? Is something wrong? How do you know? Think! Write a few notes...

_____
_____
_____
_____
_____
_____
_____
_____
_____
_____
_____.

How do you recognize what's wrong? For me it was "Panic". What is it for you? How do you recognize it? Think! Write a few notes...

_____
_____
_____
_____
_____
_____
_____
_____
_____
_____
_____
_____.

I struggled with coughing, trouble breathing and ultimately a "PANIC" Attack. Have you had an experience like this? Something that showed you something was wrong, a highly noticeable, attention getting hint? Think! Write a few notes...

_____
_____
_____
_____
_____
_____
_____
_____
_____.

I was offered a self-reporting Test on ADD/ADHD after I asked a pastor friend a few questions. Have you asked for help other than going to a doctor? Have you sought help from God? Think! Write a few notes...

_____
_____
_____
_____
_____
_____
_____
_____
_____.

I looked for spiritual help and guidance from God. I tried to refocus as I took some time and went through the 12-Step Plan in the context of Scripture. THE KEY: I WENT TO THE WORD OF GOD. It was the beginning of a new journey within

Pickin Up the Pieces of Your Life

my already incredible journey with Christ. Have you gone to the Lord for help? What did that look like? Think! Write a few notes…

_____
_____
_____
_____
_____
_____.

I went to Jesus first and then to the doctor. Have you done this? Do you realize how much guidance Christ can give you? Think! Write a few notes…

_____
_____
_____
_____
_____
_____.

Since the events of 2007 and on I have never taken medication for anxiety issues. The Lord sent me to doctors who helped me with knowledge and understanding…and that led me to the next steps the Lord had for me. How about you? How has God used others in your life? Think! Write a few notes.

_____
_____
_____
_____
_____
_____
_____.

Look at your answers. Think and pray about them? Is Christ first, second or third in your life? Considering my experiences, have you learned anything about an experience you are having or have had? Can you apply any of what happened to me, my response to my life, to your life? Think! Write a few notes...

_____
_____
_____
_____
_____
_____
_____
_____
_____
_____.

CHAPTER TWELVE

"ANXIETY SOLUTIONS"

A Personal Perspective

In 2007 I was trying to figure out what was going on with my life. If I had paid attention and could have recognized the pre-panic attack symptoms, that would have helped. I began to probe more into what was occurring, and began to get a handle on a few things. My primary focus was in the spiritual realm. I knew God had been faithful before and He would be faithful again. I was in a battle and one that seemed different than before, but eerily similar. Make sense?

I was anxious and was starting to understand what that meant and what it looked like. My family doctor helped because we began to eliminate potential problems. When I went to the emergency room a second time, they still did not say I was experiencing a panic or anxiety attack. I am not being critical of the doctors at all. They looked at it through their eyes and were wondering as well. It was a crazy time, but I was starting to figure this out. Let's move ahead through the balance of 2008 into 2009.

I was listening, reading and thinking. I took the ADD self reporting test that a pastor friend of mine had given me and I began to understand a bit more. What should I do next? I know there are many people in this country and around the world who have had and are having experiences similar to mine. From the beginning I spoke healing scriptures into my life, but to be effective in this regard I had to believe and have faith. My faith was being contaminated with fear. My faith in God was strong, but my faith in being healed and made whole, was not effective.

I worked through my situation throughout the day, but when evening came I felt as though the walls of the room I was in were collapsing on me. There seemed to be a cloud hanging over me. I was depressed! Me? Yes, Me! I recognized it! That darkness I had heard people talk about I was experiencing and it was pronounced. This is not fun, it is Spiritual Warfare. There are no anxiety disorders or phobias whether temporary or long term that come from the Lord Jesus Christ. The truth is I was getting beat up. When you are in the middle of a battle you have to get your bearings. There is a fog of war that overcomes you...but you have to get clear vision so you can determine the next step.

*****

I told you that I was in the Word, speaking healing scriptures and reading biblical texts, (Rom 10:17). My faith was getting stronger and I knew this was where my answers would be found. But war is war and the armor and tools of war you use have to be used with faith and understanding. I had fought other battles before, but this was different. Maybe the battle was not all that different, but I was different, older in the Lord and more aware of evil and what was mine in Christ.

I was doing better in 2009 and then I had a series of panic attacks in the spring of the year, just one year later to the week from the date of my first panic attack. As I read and prayed, one of the books that helped was (Prayers for the Twelve Steps; A Spiritual Journey, RPI Publishing Inc. 1993). A work book accompanied it and I worked through week one of the book. I wrote all over that first Chapter and scribbled Scripture verses in key places. That one chapter kept me moving in the right direction. As mentioned earlier in the book, I did not need nor seek AA to be delivered from my alcohol addiction, but at this time I found this Twelve Step concept to be a worthwhile journey. I found the integration of Scripture into the steps was real and effectively powerful...I took advantage of it.

I can only tell you what I did and would do again as God worked through this with me. He left indelible marks on my life through this process and one of the most indelible concerned the brain I had been given. Everything we do in life has participation from the brain, everything.

*****

As I was working through this process I found another book that profoundly impacted my life; (Battle of the Mind: Winning the Battle in Your Mind, by Joyce Meyer, 1995, Faith Words Publishing). When I read this book it seemed as though she had been reading my mind. I know that sounds odd, but it is true. She talked about the importance of the mind and its place as a battlefield. There is encouragement about staying positive, persevering and she even mentions "thinking about what you are thinking about." When I saw that and I had been saying that very same thing without reading her book, I knew we were on the same wave link in regard to this topic. In the book she talked about the conditions of the mind and the wilderness mentalities. Joyce noted that Almost 100% of us have certain issues with our thinking, though different than someone else, we still do things a certain way in our mind, we are uniquely unique. She used biblical references and spiritual insight with recommendations. She encouraged taking responsibility for our thoughts and actions as a result of our thinking. This is a good book! For those who realize they need a mental tune up and one that has Christ at its center (which I did), Joyce hits a home run and I was a beneficiary of her at bat.

Dr. Don Colbert is a physician who considers and treats the whole person. He discusses the value of good eating habits, exercise, putting Christ and His Word in your life. He targets how we should communicate without being anxious, and breaking the power of worry, fear, and a lot of other unhealthy habits ("Stress Less" Don Colbert MD, 2005, Siloam Press). Dr. Colbert wrote another good book that focused on the deadly emotions that could trigger the disease process. He dealt with anger, hostility, anxiety, repressed anger, forgiveness, resentment, being unforgiving, and hating yourself, (Deadly Emotions: *Understand the mind-body-spirit connection that can heal or destroy you,* Don Colbert MD, 2003, Thomas Nelson, Inc).

Dr. Colbert always focuses on nutrition and keeping the Word of God at the center of all you do. These two books were a blessing…and they added to what the Lord had already shown me.

I was made aware of another author who had written a book asking the question ("WHO SWITCHED OFF MY BRAIN? *Controlling toxic thoughts and emotions,"* Dr. Caroline Leaf,

2009, Improv Ltd. Publishing). Her analysis of brain function, and discussion of the brain's chemical reactions to good and bad thoughts and how the eyes and ears are a gateway to the brain is enlightening. She noted that toxic thoughts and emotions are dangerous and that we are not held captive by our biology; we can change, it is up to us. She has studied the brain for many years and has worked together with neuroscientists to learn and set the groundwork for her writings. She uses the power of Scripture to demonstrate how God has a marvelous plan for us and it is one of calm and peace.

Toxic thinking has a negative impact on a person physically as well as emotionally and mentally. In this book she emphasized the connection between mind and body. That is why, when we are under stress "extreme strain on your body's systems as a result of toxic thinking" (page 15), bad things can happen to us as it did me when I was coughing, having trouble breathing and having panic attacks. She presents diagrams that help make her points. She explains a process she calls "brain sweep, a five step process that helps a person to be free from what she calls the "Dirty Dozen" (page 14). Her brain sweep plan works. She doesn't get in the way of anyone seeing their physician, but her help adds a wonderful dimension to getting well in mind, body and spirit.

Dr. Leaf uses a lot of Scripture which demonstrates the power of God being able to help us through His Word. At the very beginning of her book she refers to the Message Bible (2 Cor10:5).

We use our powerful God-tools for smashing warped philosophies, tearing down barriers erected against the truth of God, fitting every loose thought and emotions and impulse into the structure of life shaped by Christ.

These were the books that added value to my victory over stress, anxiety, fear, doubt and depression. These books have great end notes and bibliographies which can lead you to other beneficial reading material

*****

Let's review the terms: stress, anxiety, fear, doubt and depression, the Toxic Crew as we close this chapter. There are great and lengthy narratives on stress, anxiety, fear, doubt, and depression written by professionals in the fields of psychology, psychiatry and psychotherapy. There is a manual known as the Diagnostic and Statistical Manual of Disorders (DSM) that can be useful. You may identify it by its titles: DSM I, II, III, IV, etc. This is highly sophisticated information that is the result of many hours of clinical research utilizing real people. There are books that have a lot good information that are not Christ-centered that are worthy of reading and consideration. As mentioned, I did look at other publications and books when these issues arose in my life. I *did not* treat them equal to or more important than Scripture and my faith in Christ; and what I knew and was learning through Him.

When I view this Toxic Crew I look at them as additional negative forces that arise from an out of control stressor. In other words, without us permitting stress to become a big and unwieldy force in our lives the Toxic Crew; anxiety, fear, doubt and even depression would have little fuel to operate on. I realize that a stressor becoming big in our lives is not always recognizable by the person who is suffering under its weight and pressure. I didn't recognize the stress; it took me a while to catch on and learn to respond to its effects on me. I hope this book is already helping so that you don't get blind-sided by stress and the Toxic Crew.

In the solutions category I want to share with you what I consider a wonderful answer to prayer. It really brought things into perspective for me without medication. That connection was with Neurocore®, which is a group that specializes in data driven, brain based diagnostics and treatments that help clients find their focus, improve sleep and manage stress better. I told you how I was at a July 4 Parade in 2009 when I encountered the motor home that declared the message "Reclaim Your Brain." After attending a seminar at a local seminary at which Dr. Timothy Royer explained the brain, how it works and demonstrated by using real people, many of the brain's unique characteristics and responses, I tried their program and it worked. You may go to www.theneurocore.com for more information. As I learned about the brain and its great power, I understood (Ps 139:14) more fully. We are truly fearfully and wonderfully made.

James W. Johnson Ph.D.

USEFUL EVERYDAY STRATEGIES TO DEFEAT THE "TOXIC CREW"

Spiritually: this is a Christ-centered Book. Spiritually I can only endorse one plan that has the POWER to save and heal. It is faith in Jesus Christ. I recommend following His teachings. I would begin in the Book of John in the Bible. I would go to a Christian book store and find a really good book on how to read and study the Bible and learn more about Jesus Christ. There are many strategies that people use to read through the Bible in a year, and those are found at your local Christian book store as well. There are other parts of living for Christ such as prayer, reflection, learning to love, forgive, living in the now and listening to Him and much more. Your Christian book store can be helpful here as well. Just remember, first, last, and forever "Jesus Christ is the way the truth and the life. No one comes to the Father except through Him." (John 14:6) "He never changes…" (Heb 13:8). You can count on Him."

Physically: exercise and nutrition are really important to your total well being. Yes, eating right and exercising can help you lose weight. Eating right, walking/exercising can benefit your overall health. Walking every day and keeping good thoughts will help you every day. I would just keep this simple at first. The very first thing I would do is begin to walk and do so every day. It really helps clear your mind as you walk, focus on good things not the silly and outrageous, even injurious things you hear continually on the news and from other sources. Get outside and walk when you can., it is good for your brain. Listen to good audio books that are positive or music you enjoy that makes you feel good. Second, eat well. Certainly eat meat whether beef, turkey or chicken, but I would eat more vegetables and fruit each day as well. It is best to stay away of from processed foods as much as possible. Increase those vegetables and fruits and enjoy the bountiful and vast array of colorful good foods that are rich in body building nutrients. They will help you fight disease and be stronger. You will enjoy the color and eventually you will get acclimated to the taste…you will feel better. Are eating vegetables and fruit tough for you? You can get powders or you can blend or juice vegetables and fruits to get the essential vitamins and other important nutrients they yield and the best thing is you can drink them…I recommend it! Drink more water than any other beverage and take a good multi-vitamin daily. Go to your local health food store and ask for assistance. They are qualified and will direct you to good products. This is a good start…there is a lot more but you will learn as you go. When it comes to physical and nutritional issues everyone is different; and because of medicine a person may be taking, certain foods may not be recommended.

Important message: For most people my recommendations are good, please check with your family doctor and get a thumbs up so you don't encounter any unnecessary obstacles that could stop you from successfully moving on in life.

Mental: read and do things that you enjoy, that stretch you to think and even think differently. Learn something new each day. Stay positive and stay away from negative immoral, sad and destructive messages whether on TV or online or in interpersonal relationships. You have been created to enjoy the things that are good, full of virtue and worthy of the special person you are. (II Tim 1:7) tells us that we have not been given "a spirit of fear, but of power and of love and of a sound mind."

This is part of the package we receive when we know Jesus Christ. That is Good News!

Social: get out and meet people. Don't get stuck watching TV, DVD's or playing video games, or being online for long periods of time. Enjoy the company of a good friend who is on your wave link. Renew your relationship with your spouse. Again, stay positive! Don't listen to others who are merely critical of you. Someone once said "It is none of your business what others think of you," this is good advice. You are in charge of your life. You are not a product of your biology unless you permit that to be true. Family is important. If yours is less than perfect, join the crowd. Just as we are not perfect, neither are our family members. Find common ground, show gratitude and thank God for His Goodness.

I could say a lot more on all of this. I have learned how to stay in good health in my spirit, my soul (mind, will, emotions) and in my physical body. You will too. Pray and ask God to help you. Take a few minutes daily to just listen to Him; He is talking to you all the time. Read His Word and you will learn a lot. There are wonderful answers for you, if you will reach for them.

*****

In closing the chapter on useful strategies, I am sharing with you knowledge I have received and from where I received it. Regardless of what I read or my direct contact with a physician or other professional, I have kept Christ and His Word at the center of my world. I did learn from the people and processes I have mentioned herein, but what I have learned by staying close to Jesus Christ is beyond any other knowledge of which I have been the recipient.

I want you to know that I am doing quite well. Since I started on this journey in 2007 I haven't taken any medications. As a matter of fact neither my wife nor I take any medications, period. My response to stress and the Toxic Crew of; anxiety, fear, doubt and depression has been for me to take charge of my life... *I am in charge!* I am much more aware of things around me and I am much stronger in my commitment to the Word of God and faith in Him to heal and solve problems. He gives all things to you and me to enjoy (I Tim 6:17). SO ENJOY!

Your Opportunity and Personal Invitation

Your life is important to God, your family and friends and of course to yourself. It is time to take a moment to pray. If you have never given your life to Jesus Christ, just simply say; *Lord Jesus I confess I have sinned, made mistakes and not believed and trusted in you. I turn away from my old life and receive the New Life You Offer me. I do that now. (I Jn 1:8, 9, Jn 3:16, Rom 10:13) I believe I am a new Christian; I have a New Life in You Jesus.* If you prayed that prayer you have started a New Life in Christ. Your spirit is changed and as you read His Word and fill yourself with Him (Prv 4:20-22) your life will continue to change and get better as your mind, will, emotions and your physical body absorb His Love and His Truth. If you gave your life to Christ or renewed your relationship with Him make sure you get to a good Bible believing Church and stay focused on Him. Serving Him will help you a lot as you set goals and work to improve your life. He really loves you!

CLOSING THE LOOP

In the Introduction to this book I mentioned the beginning of a loop with the promise it would be closed if you would read on. We are there and I hope that the closing of the loop reinforces your faith and courage as you move forward on your life's journey. Let's close the loop!

Recognition: It is very important for you and for me to recognize what is going on in our lives. Pay attention and daily consider what you are doing and saying. Ask yourself, how will what I am doing and saying today impact my tomorrow and the days and years ahead. If you are one who seems to be overly consumed with life and not paying attention to what is occurring in your life and how that may be impacting you and your family, STOP where you are and Think about what you are thinking about. Make decisions based on your faith in God and His Word. Take a deep breath before you take action based purely on what you feel or the situation you are in at the moment. This is from one who has not always headed that advice. (Prv 4:20-22, Proverbs) has helped me a great deal. The realization that He knows best and He never changes (Hebrews 13:8) has helped keep me on track and confront challenges in my life successfully. Again be aware, and recognize what is going on in your life.

Forgiveness: For years I wrestled with situations in my past. When I gave my life to Christ a great deal of that changed. I simply forgave those who had offended or hurt me. However, it does not end there and we must continually be willing to forgive so we don't permit someone or situation in life keep us from moving on. I believe that fear, doubt, and worry are all a part of this issue of forgiveness. Recently I had a loved one diagnosed with cancer (everything has turned out wonderfully). However, when that diagnosis was give, we began to search our souls and make sure nothing would get in the way of healing and happiness, nothing. Forgiveness was a part of that effort. In Scripture we are encouraged to forgive (Mk 11:25, Lk 17:4, Eph 4:32, Col 3:13). Over the years when I have taken offense to something that has been done to me, I haven't always responded as I should. Here is the point, unforgiveness is like a bomb. Our inability or unwillingness to forgive will ultimately detonate the bomb of unforgiveness. The sooner you let go and defuse the bomb of unforgiveness, the less you will be injured or permit your unforgiveness to hurt others. There is one Scripture that has helped me a great deal, (Rom 12:19); you see vengeance belongs to the Lord. He has the tools and the know how to take care of wrongs and hurts. This may not be easy to wrap your brain around, but if we do this as an act of love toward God and our fellow man we begin to move in freedom and the anger that inhibits us.

Gratitude: With all that you and I experience in life we may not always be thankful for the many blessings we have. Depression, mild or more severe can really get in the way of gratitude or being thankful for the good in our lives. As you read in this book, my family and I have experienced things that are not pleasant. On the other hand we have experienced blessings or God's favor in our lives. We should try to keep our eyes, ears, and all of our senses tuned to the good and virtuous things in life (Phil 4:8). There is a direct correlation between having peace and what you think about. Stay focused on the good because regardless of how tough things may be or seem to be, if you look and consider your life you have been blessed.

Career: You know that I had dreams to be an athletic trainer and as life moved forward I had other ideas and even tried some other interests to see if they may be right for me. When I was young and first married, I had people tell me that I would be a good salesman. Sales to me is building relationships and giving people an opportunity to purchase or participate in something that could be beneficial to them. I have sold many products in my life. I have been successful and as you know I have experienced failure. I have used my sales experience for many good causes and when I look at my life I know this was the direction I was to take. I didn't pursue God in this regard, it just happened. This is the point, regardless of your age ask God for wisdom concerning your career. Believe it or not, a high school or college counselor or an expert on career development may know nothing about what God wants you to do. To me this is a very important issue in our lives. It has to do with God's Favor and where He can best use you.

In (Prv 4:4-7) we are told to get wisdom and understanding and that wisdom is the principle thing. I hope you will stop right now and make sure you are putting your hands and your resources toward doing what God wants you to do. Don't chase the money; get wisdom. Make sure your career is what He wants for you. You are deployed by Him not employed by Him. His plan for you is GREAT! Take Him up on it.

Family: There was and is a plan. A Family, a unit of people; dad, mom, and children are God's plan. In life things happen; the death of a parent can change things just as it did for me. A divorce or children being born those who are not married can change things as well. In (Gn 1:27, Gn 2:24) we see this male and female becoming one. Of course there is more to becoming one than procreation. But, let's just look at things around us, and recognize, there was and is a plan. No amount of progressive thinking that we are beyond God's plan will work. We need strong families. Family units, especially those who follow the God of the Bible will have success and be blessed. This life is not perfect, we see that and we get it. But, the plan, His plan, works. We know that sound, solid, unified families, experiencing and facing both the blessings and challenges of this life, will make this world a better place, it is God's Plan.

Faith: If we are Christians today, we are often told our faith is inappropriate and a barrier to freedom in this country. Contrary to popular opinion I believe that attitude is all wrong. You can see in this book, my life and those of my family and the lives of many others that have been impacted powerfully for good by believing in and having faith in God through Jesus Christ. In (Jn 3:16) we get the message. In Jesus there is life now and eternally. "Have faith in God," (Mk 11:22), it works every time it is tried.

Citizenship: In (Mt 22:21) Jesus said we are to render unto Caesar (government) what belongs to Caesar. In everyday life we know that God can do for us and take care of us better than government...any day. Let us use our gifts and talents to create our lives and we will prosper. Government, good government by the people for the people will have in place good laws to protect and keep peace among the population of people who live in that country, state, province, city, town, county or township. A good structure that upholds the principles set forth in Scripture without restricting the personal beliefs of people works every time it is tried. I believe and it is evident that our founding documents and the signers of those documents understood what good government was and is. Nations are founded on different principles. Our country was founded on Judaeo-Christian principles. Being a good citizen is respecting that fact and helping preserve through our actions and our conversations a free nation. We are not supposed to make government our god. We have a God who extended His favor unto us. Let's support what we know is true. Let's convey our beliefs and support for our nation when we vote and how we carry ourselves each day. God shed His Grace on us. Good citizenship is recognizing that fact. We should never forget that as we welcome those who desire to come to our wonderful land to morally and legally share in its bounty.

Education: is learning. We learn through reading scriptures, literature, magazines, and other good books and studying in a more formal setting. Today there are so many opportunities to learn. We can learn from the comfort of our homes online, learn from others on the job or we can attend a school. Regardless we need to learn and often times we need to learn so that we can fulfill our career calling. Education is more than going through twelve grades. It is more than four years of college and then possibly graduate school. We have so many opportunities in a free nation to learn so that we can have better lives. I believe one should consider all the options and utilize education to improve. We only have one life to live…living it well includes a good education.

Power to Live and Overcome: It may seem simplistic, but I have found that we can live powerful and overcoming lives through a lively and committed life in Christ. In (Acts 1:8, Phil 4:13) we are being told that regardless of what is going on in life we have power and we can overcome because of the strength of Christ in our lives. I think that is the answer, you knew I would say that, right? Theologians will argue that the really good things from God will come in the next life. They will also argue that power with God is only for spiritual purposes to the exclusion of the physical. I believe that what we have ultimately after our lives are finished on this earth is going to be great and I know it will be wonderful. But our God wants to show off here and now, through us. But we have to engage Him and expect Him to do those mighty and powerful things. In (Jn 10:10, Eph 3:20, Phil 4:19,) Jesus promised life abundant the opposite of an evil one who wants to ("...steal, kill, destroy," Jn 10:10). That is here and now! I am not going to write a treatise on the power of God and the overcoming life He has for us. I am going to tell you to read for yourself in the Scripture. You will find a God who understands why He put you here and how He wants, if you will receive from Him, His power and the ability to overcome in this life. I hope you will take Him up on it.

Consistency: being consistent, doing good things over and over. It is important to be consistent staying in the Word of God daily. Eating well, exercising daily and finding productive things that keep the Toxic Crew from making headway in your life is vitally important. Don't let down your guard, stay on top of the important things in your life. Consistency will bring a certain peace as you go through each day. If I consistently write down and plan my day then doubt and procrastination are not going to get into my life. When we put things off we get behind and if we begin to worry about such things we open become vulnerable to the work of the Toxic Crew. Take a look at (Phil 4-6-8) don't let yourself get loosy goosy in regard to how you live your life. Daily watch what you think, say and do. If you are not as consistent as you should be one day, get a good night's sleep; get up the next morning, make your bed and start the day in the Word. Then be as consistent as you can be...you will never regret it.

These are key recommendations on "closing the loop." You may be able to find others and if you do, simply add them to the list.

GLOSSARY

ADD: "The hallmark symptoms of ADD are short attention span, distractibility, disorganization, procrastination, and poor internal supervision." This does not include hyperactivity (ADHD). Classic: "Primary ADD symptoms plus hyperactivity, restlessness, and impulsivity. (Based on Daniel G. Amen M.D., 2008).

Alcoholic: a person who has become personally attached to alcohol. One that has given their personal assent to and has become personally absorbed by alcohol, they believe they must have it to live. An alcoholic does not simply abuse alcohol but via consumption of alcohol permits the alcohol to be an abusive agent in one's life. (Dr. Jim's definition).

Piece: that part of one's life such as a goal, dream or desire. I use this word to describe these part's of one's life as something that did not come to pass. It was dropped on life's journey, but may be picked up bringing restoration and fulfillment to a person. (Dr. Jim's definition).

Stress: "A severe strain on your body's systems, including the brain." (Based on Dr. Carolyn Leaf, 2009).

Toxic Crew: Anxiety, Fear, Doubt, Worry, depression (mild or severe). (Dr. Jim's definition).

Anxiety: uneasiness based on an imagined or real danger. Sometimes this uneasiness takes one to the brink and panic or anxiety attacks occur. (Dr. Jim's definition).

Fear: being scared of something or somebody, Sometimes fear is based on genuine danger and sometimes apparition. Regardless, the negative effects on the mind and body are real. (Based on Dr. Don Colbert, 2003)

Doubt: "To be unsettled in opinion, or belief; be uncertain or undecided" (Websters New World Dictionary, College Edition, 1966).

Mild Depression/Depression: A personal darkness, thoughts are focused on the negative and the body is responding functionally in a negative fashion. This can be mild or hard hitting. (Dr. Jim's definition).

REFERENCE

Battle of the Mind: *Winning the battle in your mind,* by Joyce Meyer, 1995, Faith Words Publishing.

Deadly Emotions: *Understand the mind-body-spirit connection that can heal or destroy you,* Don Colbert MD, 2003, Thomas Nelson, Inc.

Magnificent Mind At Any Age: *Natural ways to unleash your brains maximum potential treat anxiety, depression, memory problems, ADD and insomnia,* Daniel G. Amen M.D., 2008, Three Rivers Press.

Prayers for the Twelve Steps; *A spiritual journey,* 1993, RPI Publishing Inc.

Stress Less, Don Colbert MD, 2005, Siloam Press.

Who Switched Off My Brain? *Controlling toxic thoughts and emotions,* Dr. Caroline Leaf, 2009, Improv Ltd. Publishing.

www.theneurocore.com

ABOUT THE AUTHOR

Jim's career has traversed the private, public and non-profit sectors. He spent many years in sales, marketing and advertising in both small businesses and with Fortune 500 and 1000 companies. He was a political consultant and a Congressional Aide working in both West Michigan and Washington D.C. His non-profit experience includes being Founder and Executive Director of Tour of Hope Unlimited and doing extensive work in major gifts, financial development, planned giving and community relations for several faith based ministries. He was the Church Administrator and Director of Small Group Ministry at a fast growing church in West Michigan. Dr. Johnson is presently serving as Executive Director of a Pro-life organization. He is also the Principal of James W. Johnson Ph.D. & Associates LLC, a consulting firm.

After a poor start academically, he went onto earn both a Master of Arts (M.A.) in Communication and a Doctor of Philosophy (Ph.D.) in Administration. He enjoys studying Scripture and reading related writings as well as biographies. He finds pleasure in physical exercise and is a two time finisher of the Chicago Marathon. He has been married to Mary for almost forty four years and is the proud father of Peter, grandfather of Eloise and Gabrielle and has a wonderful daughter- in- law Esther.

Life is most certainly more than a career and being employed. It is more than formal education and other achievements. Jim's life has been one where Jesus Christ has intervened in all areas of his life. It is noticeable how the power of God has worked and helped him succeed. He will tell anyone who takes the time to listen; *Jesus Christ is the answer for everyone who lives on this planet.*